NOW

IS THE TIME FOR

TREES

NOW
IS THE TIME FOR
TREES

Make an Impact by Planting the Earth's Most Valuable Resource

Dan Lambe
of the Arbor Day Foundation

Written with Lorene Edwards Forkner

Timber Press • Portland, Oregon

This book is dedicated to tree planters—those who get their hands dirty and believe in the power of trees to make a difference in our lives.

Published in 2022 by Timber Press, Inc.
The Haseltine Building
133 S.W. Second Avenue, Suite 450
Portland, Oregon 97204-3527
timberpress.com

Printed in China

MIX
Paper from responsible sources
FSC® C104723

Design by Hillary Caudle

ISBN 978-1-64326-106-5

Catalog records for this book are available from the Library of Congress and the British Library.

CONTENTS

THE POWER OF TREES

I grew up in a house with a massive pin oak just outside our front door. The branches on that tree seemed to reach out forever, covering almost every square inch of our front yard. Standing 70 feet tall, it was the largest tree in the neighborhood by a long shot and dominated the landscape. The trunk of the tree was enormous, and its branches dropped thousands and thousands of acorns on our lawn. It was a beautiful tree. It shows up in hundreds of old family photos, as it should, because it was part of our home, part of our neighborhood, and part of our lives.

As a child growing up under the canopy of this beautiful tree, I never fully appreciated just how important it was. I took for granted all that this tree did for me, my family, and my community. I didn't think twice about the shade it cast, blocking the late afternoon sun from our house and providing relief from the heat on hot summer days. I sure didn't consider the amount of rain our tree captured and slowed during thunderstorms, preventing floodwaters from rushing down our street and into our neighborhood storm drains. And I didn't appreciate the habitat and nourishment that oak created for the songbirds and squirrels that gathered regularly in our yard. Frankly, I took this beautiful hard-working tree for granted. It was easy to do—I was a kid. I had lots of other critical things on my mind like getting to school, heading to my next baseball practice, and riding my bike with friends.

Like that giant oak in my front yard, trees are often overlooked and underappreciated. They are a humble and reliable force in our communities that bring beauty and benefits aplenty to our everyday lives. Trees promote and protect the necessities of life. They also create unmatched beauty in natural forest lands and dense urban centers. Trees are a universal good. It doesn't matter where you live, your religion, your political affiliation, or how old you are. People love trees. As a matter of fact, in this highly divisive and contentious time, trees are about the only thing we can all agree on. Trees connect communities, cultures, and generations. They unite us in creating a positive bond of progress. Trees are amazing, but they often don't get the credit they deserve.

Fortunately, that mindset is changing. Like my coming to realize the value of the pin oak outside my childhood home in Lincoln, Nebraska, today the world is beginning to recognize the vital importance of trees and forests, the benefits they provide, and the urgency of preserving and protecting them.

Trees are under pressure like we have never seen before due to the increasing frequency and severity of natural disasters, historic forest fires around the world, and excessive temperatures soaring in our cities. At the same time, however, trees and forests are now recognized as the number one nature-based solution for reversing the negative effects of a changing climate.

That is why we at the Arbor Day Foundation say, if ever there was a time to be planting trees, that time is now. If ever there was a moment to engage in and become a part of the positive and inspiring solution of tree planting, that moment is now. This is truly the time for trees.

Lorene Edwards Forkner and I wrote this book to deliver an uplifting message about the power of trees and to encourage you to plant a tree and make your mark. In the chapters ahead, you'll read about how trees shape our lives, the essential role trees play in providing sustainable and resilient forests and urban canopies, and how you can engage in local and global efforts to plant trees. And when it's time to plant, we'll help you decide what, where, why, and how to plant trees to ensure they provide generations of beauty and benefits.

I am proud to be a tree planter. I've made a career out of encouraging and inspiring others to plant trees—and it is a pretty great job. As president and chief executive of the Arbor Day Foundation, I have the privilege of meeting forestry leaders all around the world, from the most distinguished scientists to humble neighborhood volunteers. Their heroic work motivates me. I hope *Now Is the Time for Trees* offers you the inspiration and the information you need to become part of the tree planting movement.

The pin oak in front of my childhood home is still thriving today. It stands tall like a beacon of strength dominating the neighborhood skyline. Every now and then when I drive by to see it, that tree brings a smile to my face because of the memories it triggers, the benefits I now recognize it provides, and the beauty it displays in its modest grandeur.

This is an exciting time for all of us, and we appreciate your willingness to become a champion for trees. This is the time for trees, and it is your time, too.

—Dan Lambe, President and Chief Executive, Arbor Day Foundation

ACKNOWLEDGMENTS

I get to talk about trees every day, but this is the first book I've written about them. It takes a team for an undertaking like this, and many people have made this book possible.

Let me start with Lorene Edwards Forkner, my collaborator in writing the book. To say Lorene is passionate about trees is a gross understatement. She brought her artful use of language and genuine love of trees and nature to these pages, and I am immensely grateful for her partnership.

Elizabeth Lattanzio played an irreplaceable role in making this project a reality. Her optimism, solution-oriented mindset, and sense of humor kept us all in line, on time, and laughing along the way. A true professional, she has a tremendous capacity to just get things done. Thanks for your patience, Liz.

Stacee Lawrence with Timber Press was instrumental in helping to cast a vision for what this book could be and why it is important. Many of Stacee's skilled colleagues worked to fulfill that vision.

I get to work with truly gifted team members at the Arbor Day Foundation. I am humbled by their talents and positivity. Thanks to Woody Nelson for the encouragement to move this project forward. Woody has a lyrical way with words and was important in crafting the tone for the book. Pete Smith is one of the smartest people I know, and his unique skills and knowledge were critical in helping to provide accurate information for our readers. Michelle Saulnier is a wonderful leader who plays a vital role keeping me in check at work, including during the creation of this book. I am grateful to the many other team members who pulled together information, images, and content to make this book possible, with special thanks to Lindsey Sullivan, Ashley Stephan, and Leslie Weldon for their assistance in editing. Finally, I want to acknowledge Matt Harris for providing extraordinary organizational leadership while being a great collaborator and friend.

I want to thank my wonderful wife, Brenda, and my children, Dylan and Regan, for supporting me. They offer me patience both when I'm away planting or talking about trees around the world and when I'm at home. Thanks for encouraging me, making me smile, and helping me keep everything in perspective. These are a few of the reasons why I love you.

Thanks to my mother, Liz, and father, Bernie, for instilling a tree planter ethic in me—even if I did complain once or twice about planting so many trees as a kid.

Finally, thanks to all the tree planters out there who I've had the chance to meet, plant trees with, and be inspired by. You make my job awesome, and I am so thankful for what you do.

↑ The author with his parents and years later with his own family at Arbor Lodge.

CHAPTER 1

HOW TREES SHAPE OUR LIVES

Trees play a pivotal role in the memories and story-board of our lives. From an early age to the wisdom of our elder years, trees frame our experiences. We recall them as part of the most uplifting and important events along our journeys. ▶

↑ Majestic trees often take center stage in a landscape, like these southern live oaks (*Quercus virginiana*) reaching far beyond where they started.

They shape the neighborhoods we grow up in, the parks we retreat to, the playgrounds we learn in, and the forests where we relax and explore. Our personal storyline may bend, change, even roam from time to time. Yet quietly, humbly, and sometimes majestically, trees are steadfast characters in the backdrop of our lives.

Without saying a word, trees tell us so much about a place. No matter where you go in the United States, you'll know where you are by the types of trees that surround you—from towering redwoods in the West to amazing moss-covered live oaks in the South. One of the coolest things I get to do as I travel for work is meet with other "tree people," who always want to show me the oldest, biggest, or most iconic local trees. I love it. The southern live oaks found in places like Jacksonville, Savannah, and Baton Rouge are some of the most emblematic and unusually beautiful trees you will ever see, with branches stretching out like arms, reaching to create truly wonderous tree canopies. Seeing these trees, I can't help but appreciate their history, endurance, and the comforts they provide. Significant trees like this can be found all around the nation and the globe and they all have a great story to tell.

Every tree—whether it grows in a national park, a rain forest, or in your neighborhood—is helping to provide the necessities of a good and healthy life.

GIANTS IN TIME

Certain iconic trees have inspired people for generations. As witnesses to history, these ancient trees offer a perspective that extends far beyond our lifetime and enlarges our world. There's a dignity and a grandeur to these trees that emboldens an appreciation for legacy and resiliency in us all.

Of the approximately 3 trillion trees on Earth, standing 380 feet tall and still growing, a coast redwood known as Hyperion is recognized as the tallest living tree in the world. It was discovered in a remote area of Redwood National Park in Northern California in 2006. Its height was verified by Stephen Sillett, an American botanist specializing in old growth forest canopies, who estimates Hyperion is around 600 years old.

Just 427 miles away in the Giant Forest of Sequoia National Park in Tulare County, California, is the largest single-stemmed tree in the world. Known as General Sherman, this giant sequoia is 275 feet tall and has a trunk circumference of nearly 103 feet at ground level. This stately tree is estimated to be several thousand years old.

Growing at an elevation of nearly 10,000 feet in the White Mountains of central California, a 4853-year-old bristlecone pine known as Methuselah could well be the world's oldest non-clonal tree. Even when gnarled and stunted by lack of water, extremely durable wood allows bristlecone pines to survive harsh conditions with an astonishing capacity to endure.

Halfway around the world in Sweden, the root system of a Norway spruce known as Old Tjikko is estimated to be 9562 years old. For thousands of years the tree's layering growth habit has produced trunks that die and regrow over and over, while the tree's root system has remained intact. A stunted shrub

→ Hyperion, a coast redwood (*Sequoia sempervirens*), is recognized as the tallest living tree in the world.
→ (opposite) General Sherman, a giant sequoia (*Sequoiadendron giganteum*), is considered the largest single-stemmed tree in the world.

← An ancient bristlecone pine (*Pinus longaeva*) in Inyo National Forest, where Methuselah lives.

↓ The root system of Old Tjikko, a Norway spruce (*Picea abies*), is estimated to be more than 9500 years old.

↑ The Angel Oak is a centuries-old live oak (*Quercus virginiana*) in Charleston, South Carolina.

formation, shaped by continual exposure to freezing winds, allowed the tree to further withstand the harsh conditions on Fulufjället Mountain. When the climate began warming in the 20th century, however, Old Tjikko sprouted a tree-like form more typical of a Norway spruce. The current visible tree is about 16 feet tall.

The Angel Oak in the Lowcountry of South Carolina is estimated to be around 400 years old. Native to maritime regions, live oak is known for having a broad crown and a relatively low profile that allows it to withstand forceful coastal winds. The ancient, outstretched limbs of the Angel Oak create a canopy that provides shade to nearly 2000 square yards of the land below its branches. And at 65 feet tall, the tree has achieved an impressive height as well as an astonishing spread.

A witness to history and culture, the Angel Oak stands on what was once Cussoe Indian tribal land before its purchase in 1675 by a representative of

↑ This stand of quaking aspen in Utah is actually a clonal colony of just one tree.

the British Crown. It was later transferred in a land grant to a wealthy man who owned several slaveholding plantations. According to local legend, the protective spirits of former enslaved people occasionally still appear around the Angel Oak. During segregation, Black families gathered to socialize and picnic beneath the tree's enormous boughs, a safe and respected space. Today the majestic tree is the focal point of Angel Oak Park, owned by the city of Charleston and treasured by locals and tourists alike. In 2013, the Lowcountry Land Trust purchased 17 acres adjacent to the park to protect the tree from the impact of development.

It's easy to see how visitors to Fishlake National Forest in south-central Utah might mistake the tree known as Pando for a forest. However, genetic analysis has revealed something quite different. The 108-acre stand of quaking aspen is actually a clonal colony of a single male tree with one massive underground root system. Pando (Latin for "I spread") is estimated to be one of the largest, most dense living organisms ever identified, weighing nearly 13 million pounds. The exact age of the clone is difficult to calculate, but scientists believe the tree sprouted from a single seed several thousand years ago. Unfortunately, under pressure from drought, disease, beetles, and browsing wildlife, Pando is showing signs of decline, with little juvenile and midstory growth replacing dying trunks.

MEMORY AND INSPIRATION

When planted in celebration of a baby's birth, a marriage, or the formation of a new family, a tree is a meaningful expression of growth and hope for the future. It was just over 17 years ago that we moved into our new home. My wife and I planted trees with our young kids to commemorate the occasion and literally put down roots. It was especially memorable because my parents and grandmother were on hand to help, adding to the significance of those trees.

Due to their longevity and resilience, trees also inspire recovery and healing. The act of planting a ceremonial tree is a dignified response to challenging circumstances. The living tree offers tangible proof of survival.

This American elm (*Ulmus americana*) survived the Oklahoma City bombing.

A vibrant, beautiful tree benefits everyone in this lifetime as well as the generations to come. Perhaps the most fitting memorial of all, a tree is a living remembrance that grows more wondrous with the passage of time.

Planting a tree to mark a milestone is not the only way a tree takes on special meaning. Existing trees can unexpectedly emerge as symbols of hope and inspiration as well.

THE SURVIVOR TREE

On April 19, 1995, in the heart of downtown Oklahoma City, an American elm witnessed one of the worst terrorist attacks ever to take place on American soil. Situated across the street from the Alfred P. Murrah Federal Building, the tree was completely exposed to the full force of a 4000-pound bomb that killed 168 people and injured hundreds more.

The 9/11 Survivor Tree now grows at the site of the memorial in lower Manhattan.

Shattered and broken, the tree was slated for removal to accommodate the recovery of shrapnel and evidence embedded in its trunk and branches. After the blast, however, something shifted in the hearts and minds of Oklahoma City residents, and the community came together to save the tree. The Survivor Tree, as it came to be known, stands today, a living monument in the Oklahoma City National Memorial, a symbol of hope, recovery, and life.

THE 9/11 SURVIVOR TREE SEEDLING PROGRAM

In October 2001, a month after terrorists attacked the World Trade Center in New York City, recovery teams discovered a severely damaged Callery pear buried in the rubble. Though broken and burned, the tree showed signs of life. The 9/11

Survivor Tree, as it came to be known, was extricated and handed into the care of the New York City Department of Parks and Recreation. In 2010, the rehabilitated tree was planted on the plaza of the 9/11 Memorial & Museum. With smooth new limbs emerging from gnarled old growth, the tree stands as a testament to resilience, survival, and rebirth.

Each year, the 9/11 Memorial & Museum shares seedlings grown from the Survivor Tree with communities around the world affected by tragedy. The program was launched on September 11, 2013, in partnership with Bartlett Tree Experts of Stamford, Connecticut, and John Browne High School in the Flushing neighborhood of Queens. In 2020, seedlings were donated to five hospitals throughout New York City's five boroughs as a symbol of resiliency and hope, to honor healthcare workers' response to the coronavirus pandemic.

THE TREATY OAK

On a small downtown lot in Austin, Texas, stands a majestic Texas live oak. The tree, estimated by foresters to be about 500 years old, is the only surviving member of the Council Oaks, a grove of fourteen trees that served as a sacred meeting space for Tonkawa and Comanche tribes prior to European settlement. The Treaty Oak attained national status in 1927 when it was

The Treaty Oak can be found in a small park in Austin, Texas.

determined to be the most perfect example of a North American tree and inducted into the American Forestry Association Hall of Fame.

In an act of vandalism borne of unrequited love, in 1989 the tree was intentionally poisoned with a hardwood herbicide. In fact, the vandal used enough of the toxin to kill a hundred trees. Austinites were outraged and rallied to save the historic tree, including billionaire and philanthropist Ross Perot, who wrote a blank check to fund remediation efforts. Roughly two-thirds of the tree succumbed, and arborists weren't optimistic about its survival. But, defying all odds, the tree recovered and began producing acorns again in 1997. Today, saplings grown from those acorns are sold and planted throughout the city, a testament to culture, history, and community engagement.

EVERY TREE COUNTS

A compelling and ever-growing body of evidence generated by scientists, healthcare professionals, conservationists, humanitarians, and both public and private corporations supports the critical importance of trees. Their work highlights the real impact trees have on the human condition.

Trees filter pollutants out of the air and water and provide protection for people and communities from dangerous heat and flooding. They

Start children young and you'll grow a tree planter for life.

The trees we plant today will be the giants of tomorrow.

Community Tree Recovery Program

Trees play a vital role in our communities, so when natural disaster strikes, the loss of trees can be devastating. Houses and buildings are covered by insurance, but trees are not.

The Arbor Day Foundation's Community Tree Recovery® program began in the wake of Hurricane Katrina in 2005, when an estimated 320 million trees were lost in the Gulf Coast states. The Arbor Day Foundation works with local partners on the ground to help organize tree distribution and planting events, ensuring that trees are delivered at the right time when the community is ready to replant. Since the program began, more than 5 million trees have been distributed. When tornadoes hit Alabama, Kentucky, Missouri, and Nebraska, when wildfires raged through Texas, Colorado, California, and Alaska, when Superstorm Sandy destroyed tree canopies in New Jersey, the Arbor Day Foundation was there, distributing trees, raising spirits, and renewing hope.

Over just five days in August 2016, 20 inches of rain fell on Baton Rouge, Louisiana, causing catastrophic flooding. More than 60,000 homes flooded and thousands of trees were lost. In the aftermath, aid poured in from every corner of the country and neighbors came together to help each other. But the loss of those trees seemed to crush the spirits of Baton Rouge residents, who were already facing a massive rebuilding effort. The Arbor Day Foundation understood and stepped in to help city and local leaders replace and replant the lost trees.

I have seen firsthand the emotional and ecological impact of disasters and the recovery that follows. In January 2019, I had the opportunity to be a part of a Community Tree Recovery event in Panama City, Florida. Hurricane Michael had struck the Florida Panhandle the previous October, coming ashore as a powerful Category 5 storm with winds topping 170 miles per hour. Mexico Beach and Panama City were especially hard hit, with catastrophic damage from the extreme winds and the accompanying storm surge flattening homes. Tens of thousands of trees were damaged or destroyed.

Working with state, local, and forestry leaders, the Arbor Day Foundation helped distribute trees to homeowners in Panama City and other communities in the path of the hurricane. The mood was celebratory as people of all ages—from families with young children to retirees—lined up for the chance to select a tree or two to take home and plant in their yard. Seeing their passion and excitement was both humbling and inspiring. Planting trees was the start of bringing hope and healing back to their lives.

At home and abroad, the Arbor Day Foundation works with local partners to help replace lost trees in the wake of a disaster.

↑ To plant more trees, we need more tree planters.

lower urban temperatures, reduce energy bills, and sequester carbon to slow the rate of climate change. Forest resources around the globe help to keep people out of extreme poverty.

Natural environments filled with trees and green plants create vitality and support health and well-being. These are trying times. We're stressed out, and it's making us sick. This, in turn, places pressure on our healthcare system, the productivity of our economy, and the resiliency of our social connections. More importantly, when we aren't operating at a hundred percent our energy and human potential can be curtailed, causing us to draw into ourselves rather than reach out, connect with, and strengthen our communities. A walk in the woods helps us clear our mind and has been proven to effectively counteract the negative mental and physical side effects of toxic stress. What's more, trees bring communities together.

Whether growing in a backyard, city park, national forest, or tropical rain forest, every tree on this planet is working hard to provide the necessities of life. Every tree counts. When you plant a tree in your yard, that tree immediately goes to work filtering out pollutants, intercepting stormwater, and capturing carbon. With proper placement, that tree can also help lower household energy use by as much as 20 percent. And as your tree grows, its benefits grow as well.

Planting a tree is a hopeful act—it means you believe in the future. Whether you're planting in a personal landscape, pitching in to create

Planting the Future—
With Roots in the Past

SOLEDAD O'BRIEN, journalist

When I was growing up, my favorite tree was a beautiful weeping willow on my family's property on Long Island, New York. That willow was probably the first tree I could identify. We had a lot of different trees in our yard—dogwoods and Japanese maples, to name a few—but I loved the beauty and grace of the willow.

Over time, our back yard also became a suburban forest of pine trees, the happy result of our annual live Christmas tree tradition. Each year, we would bring home a live pine tree with the giant root ball wrapped in burlap. We would decorate the tree and, when the festivities were over, plant it in the back yard. In hindsight it seems like a crazy tradition because we had to dig a hole in the frozen soil of a New York winter. My parents sold that house some years ago, but I have been back to visit, and the trees are still standing, living reminders of our family's history. It's pretty awesome to see the trees I helped plant. My parents knew we were planting for the long haul.

Planting a tree says you believe in your home or community—for today, tomorrow, and for years to come—because it takes time before you start reaping the benefits of a tree's canopy and shade. As a reporter, I cover a lot of stories that deal with inequality and communities that have been overlooked. You can learn a lot about a community by simply counting the number of trees in it. Those with plentiful trees are the communities that have historically been invested in; those where no one has bothered to plant a tree are the communities that have been ignored.

Trees, especially in an urban environment, can change the entire look and feel of a street. If you can't pinpoint what makes a particular street seem a little more magical than others, try looking up at the trees. In my neighborhood in Manhattan, 22nd Street is that magical street. When I'm walking home I often opt for the scenic route down 22nd Street because it is lined with magnificent trees.

My parents passed away a couple of years ago, within 40 days of each other. I planted three weeping willows in their memory, and we scattered their ashes around those little trees. I wanted to pick a place that I knew that they would love for their final resting spot. A tree is forever.

community green space, or supporting reforestation around the world, planting trees is both inspiring and empowering. However, to plant the number of trees that are needed to furnish a healthy tomorrow and turn the tide on the negative impact of canopy loss, urbanization, and a changing climate, we need tree planters. A *lot* more tree planters.

THE IMPACT OF 100 MILLION TREES

If one out of three people in the United States each planted one tree, the compounding benefits of those 100 million trees would be immense. According to a study by the U.S. Forest Service, over a hundred years, those 100 million trees would:

- remove 578,000 tons of chemical air pollution—enough gaseous chemical pollution to fill seventy Goodyear® blimps;

- remove 15,850 tons of airborne fine particulate matter—enough airborne particles to fill nine Olympic-sized swimming pools;

- sequester 8 million tons of carbon—equal to taking 6.2 million cars off the road for a year; and

- absorb 7.1 million cubic meters of water runoff—equal to each person on Earth filling a bottle of water every day for 5 years.

Trees clean our air and water, moderate global warming, help prevent flooding and erosion, improve our health, enhance our communities, and beautify our world. By planting more trees, this proactive, positive change can be ensured. The trees we plant today will serve our planet and its people for generations to come.

A GROWING MOVEMENT

The natural world is under pressure. The atmosphere is heating up, artic ice is melting, and species extinction is accelerating. We're losing precious soil to erosion. Hunger is on the rise, and people are suffering. It would be so easy to give in to despair. Instead, there is reason to hope. Trees are a powerful, efficient, and cost-effective tool that can be used to repair and restore the planet's damaged environments. We can plant change.

Trees are an effective nature-based solution to tackling climate change

A Viral Tree Collective— The Power of Many

MRBEAST (JIMMY DONALDSON),
YouTube creator and co-founder of #TeamTrees

What's special about trees? Well, for starters, I breathe their air!

It was actually a fan of mine who came up with the idea that I plant 20 million trees for #TeamTrees. I reached out to Mark Rober to help me figure out how to do it—I mean, he helped build a rover that landed on Mars, right?

Turns out, it's a lot harder to plant 20 million trees than we thought. Fortunately, Mark connected with the Arbor Day Foundation. With their tree planting skills and network, the foundation could take care of planting the trees and #TeamTrees could focus on raising the money.

The campaign took off in a massive way. There's so much passion and drive for trees in the environment. Every YouTube creator we pitched to was like "Cool, I want to help however I can." The youth were on fire for this project. #TeamTrees gave them an outlet for getting involved and feeling like they could make a difference. And, for others who weren't as environmentally aware, it was a great way to help bring them up to speed.

One of the funnier parts of the campaign was watching people compete for top spot on the leaderboard. It was pretty amazing to see Elon Musk donate $1 million only to have Tobi Lütke take the lead by donating $1 million plus $1.

#TeamTrees is a great example of people in the YouTube community, like Mark and me, using our connections to do something good and take it viral. We're not done. We've got more environmental actions planned for the future.

Inspired by a collective sense of urgency, a global movement of champions for tree planting is emerging and quickly gaining momentum. To move the needle, though, we need to act on a massive scale. Worldwide, we need to plant millions of trees today to have a measurable and lasting impact on billions of lives tomorrow.

→ MrBeast (right) and Mark Rober at a tree planting event for #TeamTrees.

PLANTING CHANGE: #TEAMTREES

What started as a social media post quickly turned into a global force of—and for—nature. #TeamTrees began when a fan challenged YouTube star MrBeast (Jimmy Donaldson) to plant 20 million trees to celebrate reaching 20 million subscribers. MrBeast accepted the challenge and quickly joined forces with fellow YouTuber and ex-NASA engineer Mark Rober to launch an ambitious tree planting campaign for the internet age. Together with the Arbor Day Foundation, they formed a super-team of 600+ YouTube creators along with their millions of fans, making #TeamTrees the largest YouTube collaboration in history.

#TeamTrees went viral with a simple call to action: Give $1, plant one tree, encouraging anyone with a dollar to "join the team." In just 56 days, more than 800,000 people from around the globe crowdfunded the $20 million target with donations as small as $1 and as large as $1 million. The effort is still growing, with donations every day since launch, sending a positive message that young people are stepping up to take concrete action to address the climate crisis and they see trees as a critical part of the solution.

This book is a love letter to the expansiveness of trees, their beauty, their dignity, their lasting and enduring presence, and the many ways in which they shape our memories and shelter our lives. But it's also a timely imperative to recognize and respect the impact and utility of trees in the landscape and an emphatic call to action.

As tree planters, we can harness the power of trees to provide a good life, a healthy climate, and strong communities. Anyone and everyone can participate—whether we're planting trees in our personal landscape or uniting collectively for the common good of our neighbors, forests, and communities around the globe. The time for trees is now. It's time for each of us to play a role.

PLANTING CHANGE:
TRILLION TREES CHALLENGE

Momentum is growing around a global call for tree planting. In 2020, the World Economic Forum launched 1t.org, an ambitious initiative to conserve, restore, and grow 1 trillion trees by 2030. This collaboration between public and private entities, including government agencies, nongovernment organizations, and the private sector, affirms that trees are the most effective nature-based solution to crises resulting from a changing climate.

The 1t.org initiative is driving ambition and aspiration around how trees and forests can be an important part of solving challenges we are facing today. The platform is designed to mobilize and empower action around reforestation, connecting funders and political supporters with on-the-ground champions to collectively achieve the trillion-tree vision.

YOUR INVITATION TO ACT

In the chapters ahead, you'll find prompts, ideas, opportunities, and suggestions for how you can plant trees and make a difference in your community. Some of these calls to action will be simple, some will be more aspirational. My goal is to get you thinking about the expansiveness, utility, and power of trees. Every tree counts. You can make a difference.

CHAPTER 2

CHAMPIONS FOR TREES

I t's said that a million trees were planted that day in 1872.

Farmers, homesteaders, and townspeople across the state answered the call proclaimed by the Nebraska State Board of Agriculture that a holiday be set aside to plant trees. It was the first Arbor Day. The idea struck a chord, and soon neighboring states followed suit, then every state in the nation. Why? Because trees are important. ▶

One hundred years later, the Arbor Day Foundation was founded to sustain and heighten the spirit of Arbor Day with a simple unwavering mission that remains the heart of the foundation's work: We inspire people to plant, nurture, and celebrate trees.

From its humble beginning in 1972, the Arbor Day Foundation's work and impact on the world has grown. Today, we're delivering trees to nearly a million members, trees that are greening backyards, neighborhoods, and parks. But that's only the beginning. Our work continues through innovative and sustained conservation and education programs that benefit the lives of people across the globe.

At the Arbor Day Foundation, we believe in the power of people to create change. We believe in tree planters.

WE ARE THE ARBOR DAY FOUNDATION

You can't tell the story of the Arbor Day Foundation without talking about the remarkable people who work there. The culture and values of the organization show up through our team members and their unique stories. It is a community of people committed to creating positive and inspiring programs and engagement opportunities for tree planters around the world. They bring joy to their work every day.

The team is made up of people like Pete Smith, a certified arborist who leads critical thinking around our program standards and best practices in tree planting, tree care, and stewardship. For more than 30 years, Pete has committed his career to helping people plant trees and giving them the best opportunity for success.

Lachel Bradley-Williams leads our Community Tree Recovery program. She brings a hopeful optimism to her work as she collaborates with partners to help restore tree canopies in neighborhoods, cities, and forests that have been devastated by natural disasters. Lachel has a background in natural resource management and is one of the many bright lights of positivity at the Arbor Day Foundation.

Thania Avelar manages the beautiful greenhouses at historic Arbor Day Farm. Thania and her team put great care into growing, preparing, and packaging millions of trees for our members to plant and nurture in their front yards, backyards, and communities.

These are just a few of the unique professionals and inspiring individuals who make up Team Arbor Day. Our people are the spirit and soul of the organization.

CALLING ALL TREE PLANTERS

Planting trees isn't the only thing we can do to clean our planet's air and water and make the climate more livable for people. Nor is it the only thing we can do to rebuild our communities, reduce crime, spur the economy, improve health, and stir the imagination.

But it just might be the simplest thing.

Our health and the health of our planet are inextricably connected, and the simple act of planting trees benefits both. Whether you're greening your hometown or restoring forests around the world, planting trees heals the environment while simultaneously fostering a healthy future for generations to come.

In 2018, the Arbor Day Foundation launched the *Time for Trees*® initiative—our most ambitious campaign ever. Immense global challenges determined the framework for the initiative's aggressive goals to plant 100 million trees and engage 5 million tree planters in just 4 years. *Time for Trees* changed the pace of our work to restore critical forest lands and community canopies around the world, while inspiring and engaging new tree planters and partners in our mission.

We found extraordinary support for the *Time for Trees* initiative from our members and partners. The growing recognition of the need to plant trees *now* to benefit billions of lives tomorrow is an irresistible solution-oriented opportunity that resonates with people. The Arbor Day Foundation is surging forward on the momentum of the Time for Trees initiative as we continue to grow our scale of work in new areas of need globally. We are excited to be a leader in tree planting efforts around the world. It is what we do. It is what we have always done.

FINDING INSPIRATION AT ARBOR DAY FARM

There's a place where the spirit of Arbor Day comes to life. Arbor Day Farm, the birthplace of Arbor Day in Nebraska City, Nebraska, is where people come and experience first-hand the foundation's mission. Once the home of J. Sterling Morton, the originator of the holiday, the site is now a National

↑ The State of Nebraska welcomes visitors to the Home of Arbor Day.

← (previous) Children explore the canopy at the Treetop Village attraction at Arbor Day Farm.

Historic Landmark. Families and visitors from all over the globe come to the farm to explore nature and discover the expansiveness and beauty of trees.

More than 17 years ago, when I was new to the Arbor Day Foundation, my mother sent me a photo taken on a family vacation when I was about 6 years old. There I was sitting on the steps of the historic Arbor Lodge, having my picture taken with my family during a visit to Arbor Day Farm. It was a great reminder of my roots to Arbor Day, and you can bet I've replicated that photo with my own family on those same steps. My kids are proud of what I do at the foundation. That picture reminds me of the tree planting ethic that Mom passed to me and that I am passing along to my kids.

Today, the farm's family-friendly Tree Adventure® attraction with interactive exhibits, sensory experiences, and fun learning opportunities, ignites imagination in people of all ages. At the Tree Adventure's Treetop Village®, children can climb, scamper, and explore more than 3 acres of wonder high in the tree canopy above the forest floor as they navigate a series of suspended bridges and netted walkways connecting eleven tree houses. The sprawling hotel, Lied Lodge, is a respite of hospitality for overnight guests and large conferences, while conservation demonstrations and woodland arboretums established years ago throughout the 260-acre site showcase the beauty and diversity of trees.

At Arbor Day Farm, you can taste rare heirloom apples at the Preservation Orchard and get an inside look at a working tree farm producing and

↑ The historic barns at Arbor Day Farm date back to the early 1900s.

packaging millions of trees for shipment to people all across the country. Best of all, the one-of-a-kind attractions, innovative programing, and outdoor activities at Arbor Day Farm spark curiosity and prompt engagement in the foundation's tree planting efforts.

WE ARE THE ARBOR DAY FOUNDATION

The Albertson family, William, his wife Crista, and their four children, live in Alpharetta, Georgia. As a family tradition, when each child turns 13, they get to choose the destination for a family trip. When it was daughter Hillary's turn, she chose Arbor Day Farm. She wanted to learn more about trees and visit the home of Arbor Day. The trip was a hit, memories were made, and the experience made a lasting impact on how the Albertson family looked at trees.

Inspired by the visit and her father's love of trees, the Albertson family planted 10,000 trees on their farm. That was in 2011, and the family has been Arbor Day Foundation members ever since, supporting reforestation and contributing to a community tree planting effort in their hometown of Alpharetta.

William says, "In this age of virtual experiences, involving your children in planting trees is a real activity that will bring living benefits for future generations to come."

RAISING AWARENESS AND ACTIVATING CHANGE

During my time with the Arbor Day Foundation, I've been to hundreds of Arbor Day celebrations around the United States. The events come in all shapes and sizes, but one thing remains true—it's always uplifting to be around people who are optimistic about planting trees and mindful of the power of trees to do great work in the years ahead.

One especially memorable event I attended was in Grand Prairie, Texas, where the Texas A&M Forest Service gathered hundreds of children to celebrate Arbor Day. It was one of the largest Arbor Day gatherings I had ever been a part of, and I don't know who was more excited—me or the children. It was a day full of laughter and learning, as many of the children planted trees for the first time in their lives. There were a lot of dirty hands and huge smiles as they named each and every tree and enjoyed a day in the sun with their classmates. As I participate and reflect on events like this, I am always reminded of how lucky I am to have a job where I get to help inspire future tree planters for life.

Trees make our world cleaner and greener. Our collective power to effect change—at home, in our communities, and around the world—by planting trees is remarkable. Arbor Day Foundation conservation and education programs, which we'll continue to explore in more depth in the chapters ahead, raise awareness about the many ways that trees provide workable, efficient solutions to environmental and social challenges facing the world today.

Together we can create a better tomorrow through trees. From planting neighborhood trees to ensure everyone has access to healthful green space to supporting reforestation projects across the country and around the globe, the Arbor Day Foundation provides a wide variety of opportunities to engage in the tree planting movement.

Children bring a natural enthusiasm to tree planting events.

↑ The collective experience of planting trees forms lasting bonds.

← The act of planting trees instills a sense of pride and accomplishment.

WE ARE THE ARBOR DAY FOUNDATION

An Arbor Day Foundation member since 2009, CAROLYN DRY is a tireless environmental advocate and champion for trees. Carolyn founded a company whose aim is to invent new ways of building that work with nature rather than against it.

In 2013, Carolyn created the Johnny Appleseed Initiative, a nonprofit organization dedicated to planting trees at correctional facilities and camps for at-risk youth. The goal of the initiative is to provide fruit trees to underserved populations. Produce harvested from the trees is used in facility kitchens, and the excess is donated to local food banks. As an unexpected benefit of the program, some facilities have begun educational programs teaching inmates how to properly care for the trees, valuable skills they'll take with them upon their release. As of 2021, the Johnny Appleseed Initiative has delivered more than 5000 trees to at least sixty locations in Minnesota, Wisconsin, Iowa, Nebraska, Illinois, and Colorado. In the future, she hopes to provide trees to correctional facilities in all fifty states and Canada.

KATHLEEN MINARDI, of Darien, Illinois, has been a dedicated Arbor Day Foundation member for more than 20 years. She began celebrating Arbor Day in April 2000 by encouraging people to plant trees to honor loved ones who were no longer with us. Since that time, the annual event has grown to become a significant celebration involving hundreds of

THE ARBOR DAY FOUNDATION'S
Tree Campus K–12 Program

Our children are our future. Their generation will carry on our legacy and inherit the consequences of our actions. As we'll explore in the pages ahead, a good and healthy life—clean air, fresh water, thriving communities, a tolerable climate, and abundant wildlife habitat—depends on trees. It's up to us to engage and inspire the next generation of tree planters today.

Tomorrow's environmental stewards will determine the future health of the planet. Yet children today spend more of their time indoors than out. Not only is this equation bad for their health, but it also changes how they view the natural world around them. Those who grow up playing outdoors in the dirt, climbing trees, and investigating how nature works establish an abiding connection with the environment that follows them into adulthood.

Children are far more likely to grow up to become tree planters when they have had positive romping, stomping, outdoor adventures early in life. As author David Sobel wrote, "Let us ask them to love the Earth before we ask them to save it."

The Arbor Day Foundation Tree Campus K–12® program was designed with the help of national partners to meet this challenge head on by introducing children to the many benefits and wonders of trees, both inside and outside the classroom. The program encourages schools to collaborate with local forestry professionals and others to help children learn about trees, investigate trees in their community, and cultivate a lifelong respect for trees on a global scale.

↓ Today's children are the environmental stewards of tomorrow.

RAISING AWARENESS AND ACTIVATING CHANGE

↑ Lush rain forest vegetation is vital to the entire planet.

↓ Arbor Day is celebrated in Madagascar and countries around the world.

↑ Lemurs' natural habitat exists only on the island of Madagascar and some small neighboring islands.

school children. Every Darien Arbor Day includes education sessions delivered by the Morton Arboretum as well as safety tips from Darien first responders. Thanks to Kathleen, trees have been planted in parks across the city of Darien to honor loved ones.

PARTNERSHIPS IN ACTION

With projects in more than fifty countries, every day the Arbor Day Foundation connects our partners, donors, and members to strategic, high-impact, and shovel-ready projects around the world. Our focus is trees, but our work continually demonstrates that trees help solve other issues at the same time.

One great example is work being done on the African island nation of Madagascar. The Madagascar Biodiversity Partnership reached out to the Arbor Day Foundation for help in restoring rain forests that had been massively overharvested throughout the past century, affecting habitat for critically endangered native lemurs. Replanting the forests was urgently needed to bring the animals back from the brink of extinction.

Foundation members stepped up with support to plant more than 4 million trees, which in turn provided meaningful employment for the people of Madagascar. Working in tree nurseries and on planting crews helped lift them out of poverty and provided food security, education, and an improved way of life. It also instilled a conservation mindset in thousands of local citizens now involved with the important work of the Madagascar Biodiversity Partnership.

Deforestation, loss of habitat, hunger, and poverty are inextricably linked issues in communities around the world. We are all a part of a global forest economy. It's time for us all to come together to care for our world's forests, preserve tropical rain forests, and protect our planet's biodiversity. It's a heroic task, but nations, private businesses, organizations, and individuals are working together to preserve and protect existing rain forests and replant deforested areas.

Planting 1 Trillion Trees

MARC BENIOFF, Chair and CEO, Salesforce

A couple years ago, I was at the Global Climate Action Summit in San Francisco with the legendary Jane Goodall. I was telling her about the incredible work the World Economic Forum and the Benioff Ocean Initiative were doing to protect our oceans. She turned to me and said, "It's very nice what you're doing for the oceans, but what are you doing for the forests?" I didn't have an answer, but that question stayed with me.

A few months later, I saw Al Gore present groundbreaking research on reforestation and climate change from Tom Crowther of ETH Zürich. Tom's research showed how critical trees are to the health of our planet. They sequester carbon, regulate global temperatures, act as flood barriers, and more. His research indicated that 1 trillion trees can sequester 200 gigatons of carbon, an amount equal to two-thirds of the carbon dioxide produced since the Industrial Revolution. After discussing Tom's research with scientists at the Benioff Ocean Initiative, I was hooked.

I quickly realized reforestation is a practical and actionable way to make significant progress in preventing global temperatures rising above the critical 1.5°C threshold. I knew we could activate governments and businesses to set a goal of planting 1 trillion trees in the next decade. I discussed it with other scientists and business leaders, hoping to build momentum for an initiative of such massive scale. At the World Economic Forum annual meeting in January 2020, in partnership with Jane Goodall and a multi-stakeholder group, we launched 1t.org—a global movement to conserve, restore, and grow 1 trillion trees. The initiative helps mobilize the private sector, facilitate multi-stakeholder partnerships in key regions, and support innovation and ecopreneurship.

Every one of us can join this movement. Every one of us—individuals, businesses, governments, and nonprofits—can make a commitment to plant trees. Salesforce has committed to planting 100 million trees by 2030; in our first year, we reached our first 10 million tree milestone. This is an example of stakeholder capitalism in action. Businesses have to serve more than just their shareholders. They must serve all stakeholders including their employees, customers, partners, and local communities. Certainly, our planet, including the 3 trillion trees in its forests absorbing carbon dioxide, is a key stakeholder for every business and every individual. After all, who is against trees?

PLANTING CHANGE:
THE GREAT GREEN WALL

What if we could plant a new world wonder? The Great Green Wall in Africa is an epic endeavor to do just that by planting a mosaic of trees, grasslands, and vegetation nearly 5000 miles long to help restore degraded lands. The project is also feeding and supporting people living in the region. Once complete, the Great Green Wall will be the largest human-assisted living structure on the planet.

The initiative is bringing life back to the continent's damaged landscapes, while providing jobs and combating climate change, drought, famine, conflict, and migration. According to Monique Barbut, former executive secretary of the U.N. Convention to Combat Desertification, "The Great Green Wall promises to be a real game-changer, providing a brighter future for rural youth in Africa and a chance to revitalize whole communities. It can unite young people around a common epic ambition: to 'Grow a 21st Century World Wonder,' across borders and across Africa."

A CALL TO ACTION

Today, the Arbor Day Foundation is the largest nonprofit organization dedicated to planting trees—with more than a million members and supporters. We help bring the right people and partners together to do the best work with the greatest impact.

Visit arborday.org to learn the many ways you can join the tree planting movement.

CHAPTER 3

THE CASE FOR TREES

Life is changing fast. Everywhere we look, increasingly frequent and more severe natural disasters are damaging and destroying millions of trees around the world. Historic fires throughout the American West, across Australia, and in the Amazon have swept across public and private lands, disrupting critical forests and communities. ▶

Each year meteorologists report on how excessive temperatures are putting pressure on forests and communities around the globe. As cities continue to grow, the world is getting hotter and more crowded. Our climate is in crisis.

These are daunting challenges, but there is a great optimism around tree planting. Trees are much more than a nice-to-have asset: they represent an imperative strategy for tackling contemporary challenges. With so many crucial issues facing our fractured society, trees are just about the one thing we can all agree on. If there were ever a moment for people to be a part of a tree planting movement, that moment is now.

Governments, the private sector, organizations, and individuals all acknowledge the inspiring impact and the positive role of trees. It's time for *all* of us to become tree champions. By planting trees and tending to mature trees that are already in the landscapes around us, we're cultivating a healthy tomorrow, a tolerable climate, and conditions that support vibrant communities and the health and well-being of our families, friends, and neighbors.

→ Reforestation is a global priority.

PLANTING CHANGE: U.N. DECADE ON ECOSYSTEM RESTORATION

The United Nations declared 2021–2030 as the U.N. Decade on Ecosystem Restoration, issuing a worldwide rallying cry to protect and revive forests, wetlands, and other degraded ecosystems. Planting trees is at the heart of this ambitious initiative, with a goal of working alongside local people and renowned experts to get tree planting right.

A healthy planet benefits us all. Actions that we take today can help counteract climate change, halt the collapse of biodiversity, and build better lives for everyone.

RESTORING FORESTS

Forest ecosystems represent intricate connections among plants, animals, and microbes that depend on one another and resources in the environment for their survival. The relationship between soils and trees is complex and reciprocal. An interconnected web of soil microbes and roots helps trees and other plants flourish. Deforestation, wildfires, and damaging pests—anything that disrupts the forest ecosystem—contributes to the degradation of forest soils. Reforestation, however, helps sustain and improve forest soils as well as anchor the nutrient-rich topsoil in place so it doesn't erode faster than nature can replace it.

When a wildfire burns so hot that the natural seed source is gone, the forest needs us. The Arbor Day Foundation's reforestation program began in 1990 in the wake of the Greater Yellowstone Area fires, when 800,000 acres were scorched and smoke-filled skies spanned a thousand miles. The

↓ Damaging erosion following clear cuts and forest fires disrupts forest ecosystems.

↑ Today, tree professionals around the globe
are managing forests to accommodate change.

← Post-fire reforestation brings life
back to Pike National Forest.

work began on the neighboring Gallatin National Forest in a lasting partnership with the USDA Forest Service to replant trees and bring life back.

Over the ensuing years, the Arbor Day Foundation's network of partners has grown to include the National Association of State Foresters, National Park Service, and others. Collaboration with foundation members and partners has led to the planting of hundreds of millions of trees in our nation's treasured forests. The benefits include restoring critical wildlife and aquatic habitat in Oregon's Willamette Valley, returning marginal farmland back to natural forest ecosystems in the Mississippi flyways, protecting drinking water sources high in the Sierra Nevada and Rocky Mountains, and restoring forests on abandoned mine lands in Appalachia.

I'll never forget a recent visit to Pike National Forest near Colorado Springs, where the Arbor Day Foundation has planted hundreds of thousands of trees for fire recovery and watershed protection. While touring with the forest supervisor, we came upon a ridge and looked out onto an expanse of young trees, thriving for miles in all directions. It was a powerful display of the methodical work that has gone into restoring this iconic landscape and the beautiful potential of this new forest emerging.

Rain Forest Rescue Program

Economic pressure on communities around the world has an impact on forests. The Arbor Day Foundation's Rain Forest Rescue® program is an initiative aimed at helping to keep forested land intact and more valuable than some other use, such as agriculture or encroaching developments. This program has challenged us to create innovative and sustainable ways to create economic opportunities that motivate the people who live there to protect and manage their forest lands and preserve the bounty of benefits they provide.

The Rain Forest Rescue program works with communities and families to restore tropical rain forests and build better lives for the people living there by:

- Introducing sustainable practices. Educational programs teach local residents how to make a living off of the rain forest in a sustainable way. Some partners even offer microcredit funding to those who want to start a forest-friendly business.

- Protecting remaining rain forest land. Local governments receive help to convert large tracts of rain forest land to protected areas, preserving both the landscape and culture of these regions.

- Replanting forests that have suffered from years of deforestation in places like Madagascar, Brazil, and Indonesia. Tree planting efforts are underway to rebuild the lush landscape. Locals are becoming actively involved in reestablishing the rain forest canopy, restoring wildlife habitat, and creating a better way of life for the people who live there.

- Supporting shade-grown coffee farmers. Through the Arbor Day Coffee program, Central and South American coffee farmers receive economic incentives to cultivate shade-grown coffee. When coffee is responsibly grown in the shade of the tree canopy, it helps maintain fertile soil and preserves native trees and wildlife habitat. The alternative is removing trees to create sun-grown coffee farms, which depletes the soil and devastates habitat. Shade-grown farming practices protect an entire rain forest ecosystem and produce a superior coffee that's rich and full of flavor.

Rain forest protection includes practicing sustainable shade-grown agroforestry, preserving overstory shade trees, and planting new trees to maintain biodiversity.

Shade-grown coffee protects rain forest biodiversity and provides opportunities for economic security.

↑ An environment filled with trees and other plants is known to foster a healthy lifestyle.

A GOOD LIFE

Life depends on a healthy environment. Nothing can take the place of clean water, fresh air, and a livable climate. It's complicated, to be sure, but trees play a remarkable role in supporting natural systems that ensure a good life for everyone on the planet.

CLEAN WATER

Of all the benefits that trees provide, clean water may be the most significant. In a healthy watershed, trees and other vegetation, including those in wetlands near water bodies, help maintain a balanced ecosystem by regulating natural flows, absorbing and filtering rainwater, and supporting aquatic life. Plant roots also stabilize soil and help prevent devastating erosion.

Globally, forests and wetlands supply 75 percent of the world's accessible fresh water, and about 30 percent of the world's largest cities get their drinking water straight from forested watersheds. Here in the United States, forests

A **WATERSHED** is an area of land that drains into a particular body of water. All land drains into a lake, river, stream, or other water body. In other words, we *all* live in a watershed.

↑ Clean water is one of the planet's most precious resources.

← Most of the world's fresh drinking water relies on healthy forests.

Trees pump oxygen into the atmosphere.

Particulates are microscopic airborne
particles of solid or liquid matter.

cover almost a third of our nation's land but are responsible for supplying more than half of all our fresh water. While tropical rain forests cover less than 7 percent of the Earth's land surface, they play an important role in regulating the world's climate through their impact on the water cycle—the way that water continuously moves throughout the atmosphere, evaporating from oceans and surfaces, condensing and falling as precipitation, and then returning to waterways via infiltration and runoff. These vital processes depend on healthy forests.

FRESH AIR

Take a deep cleansing breath. It feels good, doesn't it? You can thank trees and green plants for that fresh air.

Through the process of photosynthesis, trees exhale the oxygen we breathe. Using the energy in sunlight, they convert carbon dioxide absorbed from the air and water taken up by their roots into sugars. Oxygen is released as a byproduct of the process, while the sugars fuel plant growth or are stored in plant tissues. Trees also clean the air by absorbing sulfur dioxide, nitrous oxides, and other pollutants. Not only that, tree leaves act like natural biological filters, trapping airborne pollutants.

Air pollution is a major cause of respiratory illness, and even short-term exposure is harmful. Those who work outside, older adults, children, and people with existing health challenges are especially vulnerable. One of the largest contributors to unhealthy air quality is concentrated traffic emissions. Although cities are filled with interesting people, lively restaurants, dynamic cultural attractions, and centers of learning, they're also filled with busy freeways and cars—just ask anyone who's been in a traffic jam. As a result, urban centers have higher levels of particulate matter, an especially damaging form of air pollution that's responsible for that all-too-familiar haze we often see hanging above a city skyline.

Some particles, like dust, pollen, smoke, and soot, are large enough to be seen with the naked eye. Other particles, like industrial, power plant, and traffic emissions, are so small they can only be detected using an electron microscope. All forms of particulate matter are unhealthy, but especially these fine particles that can lodge deep in our lungs. Reducing particle pollution, even a little bit, saves lives.

Thanks to innovation and industry regulations, air pollution in the United States has improved since 1990. We can do better, however, and perhaps the best answer to the problem is also the simplest: plant more trees. When planted alongside roads and highways, trees help offset traffic

emissions, in turn protecting neighboring communities, schools, and business districts. Neighborhood trees can even lessen indoor particulate matter levels in homes along the street.

Planting more trees is good. Nurturing those trees to maturity and tending to existing trees already in the landscape is critical to make the most of the environmental benefits trees have to offer.

← One large mature tree can remove sixty to seventy times more pollution than a small tree.

→ Trees line the highway as you enter downtown Los Angeles, California.

PLANTING CHANGE: LOS ANGELES

An effort to plant 90,000 trees is underway in Los Angeles, a sprawling metropolis of nearly 4 million people better known for its crisscrossing freeways and hazy skyline than its shade. The ambitious project promises to deliver environmental justice and equity, in part by focusing tree planting in especially hot areas with little canopy cover, and neighborhoods in South and East L.A. that stand to benefit the most from both an environmental and social perspective.

A LIVABLE CLIMATE

Carbon is a fundamental building block of nature. It's in the air over our heads, the soil beneath your feet, and in the food we eat. Carbon-based fuels provide the energy we use to cook our food, drive our vehicles, and run our factories. Carbon is essential to life as we know it.

Since the beginning of time, carbon dioxide in the atmosphere has functioned like a global insulator, helping our planet to retain heat from

the sun and keeping the climate in a safe, stable balance, one that's quite literally livable.

During the Industrial Revolution, when fossil fuels became a dependable source of energy, levels of atmospheric carbon began to climb at an alarming rate. As energy demands increase in the manufacturing of, well, basically everything, so do carbon emissions. And while energy is necessary to power life, elevated levels of atmospheric carbon are upsetting the natural balance in our environment. One person's carbon footprint may not amount to much, but, collectively, emissions from an unchecked industrialized world quickly turn into a veritable stampede.

The same amount of heat is still coming into our atmosphere from the sun, but less and less of it is escaping. As a result, the planet's climate is changing and negatively affecting

CARBON SEQUESTRATION is the process by which carbon dioxide is removed from the atmosphere and held in solid or liquid form for the long term.

Trees as Technology

MARK ROBER, former NASA engineer, current YouTuber and co-founder of #TeamTrees

The science is clear that greenhouse emissions are causing our climate to heat up. We've learned that in part from studying space, which is my background. Mercury is closer to the sun than Venus is, but Venus is hotter due to the greenhouse effect on overdrive. Its atmosphere is so hot that we can't even send a spacecraft or a probe to its surface because even our best metals would melt.

Here on this planet, we're working to offset greenhouse emissions by building new machines that suck carbon dioxide (CO_2), a greenhouse gas, out of the air. If you're looking at the best existing technology, however, it's trees. Trees are a natural carbon vacuum. First of all, they are powered by the sun. They suck CO_2 out of the air, rip the C from the O_2, slap the C on themselves to increase their mass, and then they release the O_2. It's a great deal—trees get what they need to grow, we get oxygen, beauty, and shade!

Obviously, trees are not going to solve climate change on their own, but it's important to recognize how valuable they are in our environment.

When Jimmy (MrBeast) and I created #TeamTrees along with Matt Fitzgerald, we used our influence to reach out to our friends and followers to raise money and plant trees. But, more importantly, the campaign was a way to connect with the younger generation and get them to show Mother Earth a little love: Now that you're on #TeamTrees, turn off the lights when you leave the room, recycle that plastic bottle. We only get one planet, and it's our job to take care of it. Someday these kids will have kids of their own, so hopefully this movement will have ripple effects that play on for a long time.

Planting more than 23 million trees is pretty incredible, but the real MVPs are the folks who left comments and posted their own videos in support of #TeamTrees. As they talked with friends and family and with their teachers at school, the movement grew organically. Those foot soldiers, people on the ground working to raise money and awareness, are the ones who created such a positive campaign.

living conditions around the world. As carbon dioxide levels rise, these effects worsen. Extreme heat waves cause suffering and contribute to the spread of infectious diseases. Rising ocean temperatures produce stronger and more frequent hurricanes, while in other parts of the world drought conditions fuel ravaging wildfires. This regional devastation is heartbreaking and costly and often has lasting effects. The loss of natural habitat is also negatively affecting biodiversity and threatening countless species of plants and animals.

Reducing global carbon emissions and combating the effects of climate change is an enormous challenge, possibly the greatest of our lifetime. The good news is that awareness of the magnitude of the problem is increasing. Companies and individuals alike are developing Earth-friendly renewable energy resources and technologies that remove excess carbon emissions already in the atmosphere. There's a growing movement to halt deforestation. But one of the simplest and most effective solutions to this complex problem is all around us: trees.

Forests are also central to the global carbon cycle. Through photosynthesis, the world's forests—sometimes referred to as the lungs of the planet— help keep carbon dioxide in balance by storing carbon and producing oxygen. Excess carbon not used to feed trees remains sequestered, or locked up, in the roots, trunks, and branches of living trees and in wood products after the trees are harvested. In this way trees become a valuable carbon sink. Rotting leaves, organic debris, and soil organisms also contain carbon. In fact, forests in the northern United States can sequester twice as much carbon in the soil as above ground.

A **CARBON SINK** is a forest, ocean, or other natural environment that absorbs more carbon from the atmosphere than it releases.

Trees can help restore balance, but it's going to take all of us to ensure enough of them are preserved and planted to make this new equilibrium a reality. The world needs more trees. Each and every one of us can do our part and become climate champions by planting trees at home, in our communities, and in our nation's forests.

HEALTH AND WELL-BEING

Trees also have a tremendous effect on our health and well-being. A walk in the woods benefits us—body and soul. Outdoor enthusiasts escape to the forest to hike, camp, fish, interact with wildlife, and get their fill of time among trees. For others, time spent among towering trees is an almost

↑ A hike in the woods is chance to get moving and connect with nature.

↑ Public parks and green space promote a healthy, active lifestyle.

sacred experience, a chance to celebrate and connect with nature. Whether you're in it for the exercise or simply looking to relax, spending time in a forest is refreshing and rejuvenating.

AN ACTIVE LIFESTYLE

Green spaces not only make us feel good, but they are good for us, too. Studies have shown that people who live near neighborhood parks and green spaces are three times more likely to be active and physically fit. That goes for children as well.

Being physically active is key to living a good life, and trees are a good source of exercise. Digging and planting, trimming and hauling branches, raking and bagging leaves, or stacking wood burns three to six times more

↑ Outdoor play promotes learning.

energy than reading this book. What's more, active people stay healthy and have lower medical bills, which in turn lessens the toll on our nation's healthcare system.

CLEAR THINKING

Cognition, the process by which we think, perceive, and interpret the world through our senses and relate to others, is central to our humanity. Healthy cognition helps us navigate life successfully.

Green space is powerful. How well we comprehend, solve problems, and remember is established early in life. However, noise, chronic stress, even pollution—conditions, coincidentally, that describe a bustling urban environment—can impair our ability to think clearly, often with lasting impacts. Yet simply taking a walk in a green space filled with trees and other vegetation has been shown to improve memory and boost a person's ability to concentrate and focus.

A growing body of research reveals that not only does interacting with nature help us to develop these life skills, but time outdoors in green spaces can also help to restore healthy cognition at any age. For instance, one study found that after taking a nature walk, college students received higher test scores compared to those who went on an urban hike or stayed indoors. Findings have also shown that:

- children learn better and become creative thinkers when they are active outdoors;

- taking a break in a plant-filled environment helps relieve an employee's work-related mental fatigue and improves job performance; and

- elderly adults are better able to concentrate after spending an hour resting outdoors in a garden setting.

Think of the potential impact of integrating natural green spaces filled with trees in and around schools, college campuses, workplaces, and health-care facilities. Planting trees and protecting and expanding natural green space expands everyone's opportunity to interact with nature—which, in turn, promotes healthy minds and productive learning.

STRESS AND MENTAL HEALTH

Stress is normal, inevitable, and sometimes even beneficial. Occasional challenges in daily life can inspire fresh thinking and push us to tackle problems in a new way. Cortisol, a hormone that our bodies produce in response to

The Wisdom of Trees

RUDY PANKOW, actor

I was raised in Ketchikan, Alaska, in the Tongass National Forest, running through the trees with my brothers, even when it was cold and wet. That rain forest is my childhood. From a very early age, my dad and mom taught me that trees are teachers. Patiently and humbly, they go about caring for us and contributing to our ecosystem.

These days, whether I'm at home in California or working on set among the giant live oaks back East, I go out into nature to recharge. If there's a tree that's climbable, I'm in it—I love hanging out in trees. Once when I was working on location, I held up production because I was lying in a tree and no one could find me. Being among trees, like here in the Sierras, motivates me; this is my place to think. I tell people who might not understand what I'm talking about to go out into nature, preferably alone, just to experience the beauty and powerful energy of trees. They'll get the message.

I've made it my mission to care for trees as much as they care for us. Big things matter, like really researching a candidate's environmental policies, especially regarding forestation, before voting. But little things matter too, like taking bags to collect trash when I'm hiking with my friends. I come from a place where that sort of thinking was a part of my upbringing. Not everyone is that lucky. That's why I encourage people to make the time to get out among trees and take in their steady supportive energy.

I once read a great quote, "Someday we will appreciate all the things that were never built." These places are our responsibility to preserve and care for, before it's too late.

↑ Wooded landscapes inspire wonder.

stress, fuels the fight-or-flight response and helps us respond to an immediate threat or danger. But when stress becomes chronic and cortisol levels
remain elevated, our health suffers.

Physical symptoms of chronic stress include high blood pressure, weight
gain, headaches, and lowered immunity. Mental health symptoms may present as feeling overwhelmed, nervous, anxious, or depressed, or in displays
of violent behavior. Stress and anxiety disorders are not uncommon for
people living in cities. Fortunately, as more of the world's population shifts
to urban settings, attention is being paid to how this environment affects
people's quality of life and mental health.

Urban forests, trees, and green spaces have a natural calming effect on
people living under stressful conditions. Creating verdant areas that are
accessible, attractive, and used by the greatest number of people results in
tangible public health benefits. Trees give communities a healthy counter-
balance for the stresses of daily life and provide residents with spaces that
boost their mental well-being.

Tree Campus Healthcare Program

Trees and green spaces in a healthcare environment enhance patient recovery—but urban tree cover is shrinking, and its associated benefits are often not distributed equitably. The Arbor Day Foundation Tree Campus Healthcare® program recognizes health institutions that are dedicated to fostering wellness and community engagement through trees.

The program, which began in 2019, connects inpatient healthcare facilities of all sizes throughout the United States, including hospitals, senior care facilities, and other residential rehabilitation properties, with local community forestry programs. Each participating healthcare facility agrees to commit resources, both human and financial, to maintaining the health of existing trees on the property and to develop plans for new plantings. The facilities also commit to offering community programming that informs participants and celebrates the connection between trees, nature, and human health.

In 2020 the Cleveland Clinic was recognized for their tree planting efforts, onsite as well as in and around the neighborhoods they serve. The clinic actively supports the tree planting movement as a means of creating resilient and sustainable communities, which in turn translates into healthier citizens.

"Participating in the Tree Campus Healthcare program is an integral part of our strategy to invest in the health and well-being of the population we serve," says Jon Utech, senior director of the Office for a Healthy Environment at Cleveland Clinic.

Health and wellness are the foundation of a good life. I continue to be impressed and excited to see the passion of healthcare professionals committed to integrating trees, forests, and greenspace as a way to genuinely help their patients and improve the lives of everyone in the community at large.

↑ Connecting with nature, even if it's only a view from a window, promotes healing.

HEALING

Recovering from health challenges can be a struggle. Medical treatments, surgery, and ongoing therapy can take an intense psychological, emotional, social, and economic toll on patients. It takes time to regain both physical health and mental sharpness. And the longer patients spend recuperating, the longer it takes them to return to a normal life.

Spending time in hospital gardens is beneficial in so many ways. Patients feel better and are more tolerant of medical procedures. Visiting friends and family are less stressed, and hospital employees are more productive. Garden-based therapy programs are more productive and induce less fear in patients.

In fact, just the sight of nature can have a healing effect. Hospital patients whose windows look out onto natural green space have been shown to recover more quickly and require fewer potent painkillers. Nurses record more progress, and hospital stays are shortened.

A CALL TO ACTION

Here in Lincoln, Nebraska, my office is only a block away from the University of Nebraska's downtown campus, home to a beautiful arboretum. Sometimes in the middle of a busy or hectic day, I'll simply walk over to campus to stroll through the trees. Observing and enjoying the tree canopy brings a smile to my face, helps me rejuvenate, and reset my batteries. Tree time helps me get back to work with a fresh mind and the inspiration to help plant more trees.

Find a park or tree-lined street nearby where you can take a stress-relieving walk during the day. Draw in some deep breaths, reconnect, and center yourself.

CHAPTER 4

STRENGTHENING COMMUNITIES THROUGH TREES

Becoming a champion for trees is an optimistic and social act that moves beyond partisan, religious, geographic, and all other divides. Government and nongovernment entities, scientists, actors, athletes, musicians, corporations, and everyday people are getting involved. ▶

Whether you're beautifying your landscape, helping to green your community, or supporting a forest on the other side of the world, it seems that the need to plant more trees is something everyone can agree on.

Trees foster a feeling of home. For many, the more trees there are, the more people like where they live. Tree-lined streets and residential areas with common green areas create a sense of neighborhood. Parks and open spaces draw neighbors outdoors and encourage connection. Children thrive when they have a safe space to go outside and play. Residents who live in neighborhoods with abundant greenspace are more likely to lead active lives and enjoy good health. As an added benefit, exposure to nature, sometimes referred to as "vitamin N," has been shown to encourage cooperation and positive behavior. Happy children. Happy parents. Healthy neighborhoods.

→ Trees bring splashes of autumn color to Charlotte, North Carolina.

PLANTING CHANGE: CHARLOTTE'S TREE CANOPY ACTION PLAN

The city of Charlotte, North Carolina, has a plan for protecting its trees. While the existing urban forest canopy is robust, covering about 45 percent of the city's area, the trend is one of decline. The city's Tree Canopy Action Plan is an effort to reverse that trend and preserve, restore, and enhance Charlotte's beautiful trees. Working with community leaders, residents, and local industry representatives, the Tree Canopy Action Plan aims to build consensus, create a shared strategy for protecting Charlotte's natural environment and tree canopy, and identify opportunities for growth.

URBAN HEAT ISLAND EFFECT

Let's say it's 74°F in your suburban neighborhood. Not far away in the middle of downtown, however, it can be more than 10°F hotter. That's because urban settings filled with concrete and hard surfaces absorb and re-emit the sun's heat more than a landscape filled with trees and vegetation. This creates an island of warmer temperatures relative to conditions in other areas with more canopy coverage.

LIVABLE CITIES AND TOWNS

More than half of the world's population lives in cities, and in North America that number is closer to 80 percent. This trend is going up, which is not surprising. City life has a lot going for it: a diverse population, economic potential, civic and community engagement, cultural and educational opportunities, restaurants, and shopping. Yet for all their benefits, many cities are hot and crowded.

Whether you live in a big city or a small town, energy is an essential resource. It powers our global economy, fuels our communities, and provides comfortable living conditions. As you might expect, the greatest demands for energy come from the largest urban areas. And while there are upsides to density, like less sprawl and more public transportation, as population centers grow, energy use for air conditioning and cooling does as well. This increased demand puts pressure on electrical infrastructure, which leads to more frequent or prolonged power outages and accelerates the need for costly system improvements.

Globally, heat-related stress is a serious health problem. Scientists predict that extreme summer temperatures, in the United States and around the world, will continue to rise, causing tremendous challenges including an

Trees to Beat the Heat

MAYOR REGINA ROMERO

My father was a farmworker in Somerton, AZ, and felt that working the land to feed people was honorable and necessary labor. But he was most in his element in the mountains of Mexico. We would go there to ride horses, eat in the fields, nap under the trees, and tell stories—to "learn to love the land," he would say. He grew up in a small town in Sonora, by the river, and his parents grew their own food. He used to joke with us that he was an "original organic." At age 15, he came to the Unites States as part of the Bracero program to work in the fields.

My siblings and I grew up as environmentalists and conservationists, mostly out of necessity, although we didn't realize it at the time. Reducing, reusing, and recycling—whether it be clothing or household supplies—was simply a fact of our lives because we couldn't afford to be huge consumers. Many families throughout our country, especially families of color, currently share this same reality.

Extreme heat continues to be an issue that is front and center to me, especially as mayor of Tucson. In 2020, the city experienced its driest and hottest year on record. Frontline communities are disproportionately affected by extreme heat due to the historical disinvestment and low-tree canopy found in lower-income neighborhoods.

My dad planted trees everywhere he went. Not only because they were a precious resource and protected us from the sun and heat, but also because they were a source of happiness for him. My dad was in his element when he was among the trees. Mesquites were his favorite. He always told me to "look around and plant what you see," and when my husband and I moved into our home, he stood with me in the yard and pointed out all the places we should plant trees.

That is why I launched Tucson Million Trees (TMT), an initiative that aims to plant 1 million trees by 2030 and prioritizes the most heat-vulnerable neighborhoods. My children and I planted the first TMT tree at our home in memory of my father. As my father did with me, I am showing my children the value of trees and healthy ecosystems. As a family, we will care for and nurture this tree; as mayor, I will work alongside my fellow Tucsonans to do the same for our local tree canopy across the entire city.

↑ Bryant Park in New York City draws a crowd on a sunny day.

increase in heat-related illnesses and deaths. But cooling relief is possible if we tend to the existing tree canopy and plant for the future.

Trees lower surrounding air temperature in a number of ways. In summer, when the sun is the most intense, trees reflect between 70 and 90 percent of the sun's energy back into the atmosphere, cooling anything in the shelter of their shade. Less obvious, but equally effective, cooling also occurs via transpiration, when plant roots take up soil moisture and release water vapor through the leaves, stems, and flowers. If you've ever been in a greenhouse filled with plants on a sunny day, you know how humid conditions quickly become. And as that moisture evaporates, the surrounding air is cooled.

Creating green infrastructure by planting trees and connecting urban forests, natural spaces, and waterways helps reduce energy needs, breaks up urban heat islands, and creates more livable cities. In turn, utilities use less fossil fuel to create energy, which reduces carbon dioxide emissions. When you think about infrastructure in towns and cities, built infrastructure ages and loses value, whereas green infrastructure increases in value and benefits over time. Planting trees along city streets, in parks, and around schools and businesses is an economical and winning strategy for reducing energy usage and developing urban growth that's more in harmony with nature.

→ The City of Dallas is working to vastly expand its urban forest.

PLANTING CHANGE: DALLAS'S URBAN FOREST MASTER PLAN

Thirty-seven percent of the City of Dallas is covered with impervious surfaces, making it the third fastest growing urban heat island in the United States. This situation also worsens the city's flooding and air quality issues. The health of Dallas's urban forest is also impeded by a fragmented tree canopy. Only 29 percent of the city has tree cover, and new tree plantings are not keeping pace with tree removals and mortality, adding to the fragmentation. Studies show that there are nearly 1.8 million potential tree planting spaces in the city.

The Texas Trees Foundation, working with the City of Dallas and Davey Resource Group, Inc., has launched an initiative to create the first ever Urban Forest Master Plan for the city of Dallas. The plan outlines a shared vision for preserving the existing tree canopy while also expanding the urban forest as the city continues to grow and develop.

↑ Pavement and stormwater are a costly mix and potentially dangerous.

← Trees help slow stormwater by holding rain on their branches and leaves.

STORMWATER

Rain refreshes the land and nourishes the green landscape. But as cities and towns continue to grow, they lose both tree canopy and exposed soil that can soak up moisture. When the balance tilts too much toward concrete, asphalt, and rooftops, welcome rain becomes costly stormwater runoff.

Urban stormwater runoff washes chemicals like oil, gasoline, and other toxins, as well as litter from surface streets and parking lots, into streams, wetlands, rivers, and oceans. Pollutants washing into community waterways contaminate drinking water, harm aquatic plants and animals, and can overwhelm municipal storm systems and cause dangerous flooding.

During brief, low-intensity storms, trees help reduce damaging erosion by slowing and holding rain on leaves, branches, and bark, which allows water a chance to soak into the soil where it belongs. Every patch of green space helps, and it all adds up. Breaking up parking lots to accommodate pockets of landscaping, planting street trees, and protecting mature trees in the existing urban canopy are all ways in which urban communities can manage the effects of stormwater, reduce damage, and mitigate costly storm cleanup.

Multiply the runoff-reducing effects of one tree over a whole urban forest canopy, and the results are significant.

In public plazas and shopping districts, trees create a unique and welcoming sense of place.

PLANTING CHANGE: BOISE, CITY OF TREES

Boise, Idaho, has long been known as the City of Trees, but residents aren't resting on their laurels, their maples, or their birches, either. With both Tree City USA and Tree Cities of the World recognition, the already arboreal community is committed to battling climate change with a plan to plant 100,000 trees in the next 10 years—that's one tree for every household in the city.

The city is also challenging community members to sponsor seedlings, one for every Boise resident, to be planted in forests across the state of Idaho. Boise's City of Trees Challenge is a model for communities around the United States to build climate resilience through tree planting.

BETTER BUSINESS

Trees and green space are good for business. Framing city streets and sidewalks with trees and integrating pocket parks and seasonal plantings into a business district helps to create a sense of place and a welcoming destination. Although many factors can have an impact on the overall urban economy, shoppers, diners, and pedestrians are willing to travel further and stay longer when visiting shopping districts that have attractive trees and well-maintained landscaping.

Trees play a major role in shaping a business district's identity. And a quality business landscape—one that adds beauty, increases outdoor comfort, and complements business storefronts—is good for local businesses as well as the community's overall economy. More time spent in an enjoyable green business district translates to increased spending at local restaurants and retail stores. Commercial properties with beautiful landscaping and shade trees can even command higher rents, and employers can boost worker productivity and job retention just by providing a green view.

Tree City USA Program

Trees are essential in our cities and towns. Through the years, the Arbor Day Foundation has built programs designed to inspire positive behavior and advocate for sustainably managing trees in our communities. Tree City USA®, our longest running urban forestry program, has been greening cities and towns across America since 1976. In many ways, the program has become the foundation of urban forestry management across the United States.

While attending a meeting of the U.S. Conference of Mayors several years ago, I had the opportunity to meet with mayors from all over the nation. When they heard that I worked for the Arbor Day Foundation, mayors from Miami to Las Vegas to Honolulu to Grand Forks all started proudly sharing how long their city had been a Tree City USA. It struck me how important trees were to them and to their community members. Mayors often tell me that trees are one of the things they get the most calls from their constituents about year after year.

Today, in all fifty states, Washington, D.C., and Puerto Rico—from the Gulf of Alaska to the Gulf Coast—nearly 155 million Americans are living in Tree City USA towns and cities. Tree City USA communities' range in size from New York City and Los Angeles to tiny Sibley, North Dakota, with just over twenty residents. All these communities are committed to strategically planting trees as a dynamic part of their city's infrastructure, providing profound environmental and community benefits, and bolstering pride among the people who live there. The Tree City USA program is inspiring important work in tree care and creating more beautiful, sustainable, and resilient cities.

⬆ Wooded parks provide respite in Tree City USA, New York, New York.

⬅ (far left) A town proudly posts its Tree City USA designation.

⬅ (center) Trees line the walkway of public gardens in Tree City USA, Boston, Massachusetts.

⬅ Trees shade a playground in Tree City USA, Atlanta, Georgia.

Tracking Time with Trees

ROSARIO DAWSON, actress

I grew up on the Lower East Side in New York City, but thanks to my family who loved spending time in nature, I connected with trees at a very young age. We took a lot of trips upstate to go camping and hiking, but I didn't need to leave the Lower East Side to be mesmerized by trees. Our fourth-floor apartment faced a courtyard filled with massive trees, and I loved staring out the window at them and watching their leaves turn and flip through the seasons and years.

Trees have a beautiful way of measuring time. Recently, my daughter and I visited my grandfather in South Carolina. Years ago, my grandmother Mima planted a small palm tree in their yard. All these years later, the three of us had our picture taken under the shade of that now-huge palm tree in remembrance of our beloved ancestor.

I'm so grateful for the abundance of nature I was raised in—like the Sixth Street Community Garden, where my grandmother Pena still has a plot. Walking from Tompkins Square Park (my favorite park) to the garden and down to the East River, I would pass the most gorgeous weeping willow trees at La Plaza Cultural de Armando Perez community garden on the corner of Avenue C and Ninth Street. Those trees were such a

spectacle, you couldn't help but stop and look up in wonder. The weeping willows, affectionately named Cher, Krusty, and Wally, had watched over the block since the 1970s. They were loved by everyone, making their block a gathering spot for the community. Diseased and damaged by Hurricanes Irene and Sandy, they eventually had to be taken down. The neighbors felt the loss so deeply they held a tree wake in honor of their beloved weeping willows.

Trees like those weeping willows are so important in urban spaces. Without them, you lose moisture, coolness, and shade. Dangerous heat islands are formed, contributing to higher asthma rates and other damaging health issues. Unfortunately, heat islands most often occur in poor urban areas where trees and parks are sparse. That's why I'm so moved by organizations like Bette Midler's New York Restoration Project and the Movement Generation Justice & Ecology Project in Oakland, California, who fight for equitable access to green space.

We're all on this beautiful Mother Earth, and we have to treat her right. One of the best things we can do is plant trees.

GREEN EQUITY AND ENVIRONMENTAL JUSTICE

Neighborhood design is a public health issue, as land use and zoning laws determine where polluting industries are located. Not everybody has ready access to clean air and health-promoting outdoor green spaces. Not all schools enjoy the shelter of trees. A recent study by the National Center for Environmental Assessment reveals that people in poverty are much more likely to live near polluters and breathe polluted air.

Leaders in the environmental justice movement are raising awareness of social inequities related to economic, environmental, and health issues. A satellite image of a city will clearly show the disparity of areas of lush, green tree canopy compared to areas that lack trees. That same image will often mirror the contrast of social and economic disparity in that city. Everyone deserves a safe, clean community and workplace environment. Forestry professionals and proponents for social justice are collaborating like never before to ensure that all communities have equitable access to the benefits that trees provide.

One of the most overlooked opportunities to put trees to work in our cities and towns is establishing urban orchards and food forests that provide an abundant harvest. Around the United States, creative and inventive

↓ Public green space builds strong communities.

↑ Public access to community fruit trees strengthens food security.

organizations and neighborhoods are strategically planting trees to bolster the local food supply while also respecting the heritage and culture of residents. From fruit trees on college campuses in Arizona to community gardens that supply food to local farmers markets in Boston, there is a drive to use urban agroforestry as a solution to meeting community needs. In addition to producing a generous crop, these trees are creating multiple community benefits. Increasing tree canopy and public green spaces opens new opportunities for active lifestyles, supports good health, and fosters vibrant communities.

THE FACES OF URBAN FORESTRY PROJECT

They are your friends, your neighbors, and your coworkers, and they come from communities across the country, large and small. Their stories are inspiring. These are the Faces of Urban Forestry—citizens whose lives have been changed by a community tree project or program.

The Faces of Urban Forestry project is an initiative of the Arbor Day Foundation in cooperation with the USDA Forest Service to celebrate the leadership and vision of urban forestry programs around the nation. This project has resulted in a collection of personal stories demonstrating how people benefit from federal, state, and local urban/community forestry programs. Trees are changing the lives of the people who live and work in our nation's cities and towns.

In 2011, Washington, D.C., resident Rondell Pooler signed up for the DC Green Corps training program, a decision that would help shape the course of his future. He learned about tree planting, park maintenance, stormwater management, urban agriculture, and volunteer supervision. After completing his training, he was hired by Washington Parks & People to run the DC Green Corps, his first green job.

More than 141 million acres of America's forests are located in cities and towns. Parks and gardens, landscaped boulevards, river and coastal promenades, greenways, and even simple street-side tree boxes form urban forests.

More than a decade later, Rondell continues his career in urban forestry. He divides his time between running his own landscaping, urban agricultural, and forestry company, Rooted & Sustained, and serving as a community garden specialist for the DC Department of Parks and Recreation. Rondell loves working outside and growing food for his community all while helping the environment.

↓ Trees bring vibrancy to urban environments.

Rondell says that one of his prouder career moments came when he was walking in Marvin Gaye Park in Washington, D.C., with a friend who commented on the beautiful trees lining Nannie Helen Burroughs Ave NE. He was delighted to see these were the very trees he had planted as a trainee for DC Green Corps.

When she was young, Queens native Lori Goodman Lester was drawn to animals, green grass, and trees. Recognizing her intense interest in nature, Lori's mother sent her to an ecology camp in upstate New York, where Lori nurtured her passion for the environment and learned skills she would use throughout her life.

Lori's first opportunity to test her green thumb came when her family moved to the more rural community of Great Neck, Long Island. There, she met a science teacher who shared her penchant for the environment. Together they marked nature trails on the school property, which Lori later used to teach fourth graders animal behavior as part of a gifted and talented program.

That first teaching experience led Lori to pursue a degree in education. In 2012, she was teaching at Public School MS 219 in Flushing, Queens, when Superstorm Sandy ravaged the east coast and destroyed many of the trees on the school property. The New York Restoration Project (NYRP) donated trees to replace those lost in the storm. Lori was there, shovel in hand, leading her students in their first tree planting event.

↓ Community apple trees contribute to food security.

Alliance for Community Trees Program

The Arbor Day Foundation's Alliance for Community Trees® is a nationwide network of local nonprofit tree planting organizations. These passionate nonprofits are the boots on the ground—mobilizing thousands of volunteers to plant and care for trees, particularly targeting areas where trees can help reduce the urban heat island effect, save energy, reduce stormwater runoff, and beautify neighborhoods.

With more than 80 percent of Americans living and working in towns and metropolitan areas, the need for motivated and informed local tree planting actions is greater than ever. The Alliance for Community Trees network is an integral part of making that happen by empowering these committed organizations to deliver our shared mission in the communities they serve.

Around the country, local nonprofits are planting trees today for a better tomorrow.

GREEN EQUITY AND ENVIRONMENTAL JUSTICE

Inspired by the project, Lori volunteered to head up NYRP's twice annual Tree Giveaway and distributed more than 800 free trees to New Yorkers. With additional funding from NYRP and the Queens Botanical Garden, she and her students planted more than seventy trees, including twenty apple trees, as well as gardens filled with herbs, vegetables, and pollinator plants to attract bees for their little apple orchard.

"The kids have a vested interest in the trees and plants. Whether it's making apple sauce from a tree they grew themselves or learning the proper way to prune a tree, their work in the garden always leaves them with a sense of ownership and pride," Lori observes. "Self-respect is built from seeing products that come from their efforts."

Barb Burrill is a citizen, mother, and self-described "Seattle orchard steward." When Barb noticed several abandoned fruit trees along an urban trail in 2008, she became a volunteer with Seattle Parks and Recreation, where she works to rehabilitate and care for the remnants of old orchards located in the city's parks. Next, she joined the nonprofit organization City Fruit, a model for citizen involvement in local food sources founded in 2010. Barb trains volunteers, home fruit tree owners, landscape professionals, and arborists how to prune and care for fruit trees, both public and private.

These collaborative efforts increase the availability of fresh, locally grown fruit and encourage homeowners to plant trees of their own. "Fruit trees provide a valuable food source right here in our community," Barb says. Come harvest season, the fruit is picked by City Fruit volunteers and distributed to food banks, shelters, and community organizations.

These personal stories provide a glimpse into the positive impact of urban forestry programs. Hundreds of millions of city dwellers around the world are beneficiaries of the professional and technical programs that make up the science and art of urban forestry management today. There has never been a more sophisticated approach to caring for trees in our cities, towns, and neighborhoods. This work benefits us all as we literally and figuratively live, work, and play in the shade cast by the professionals and volunteers who lead those programs.

REDUCING CRIME

A thriving community filled with trees and open green space is good for everyone. But studies have shown that in barren environments devoid of green space, a breakdown in social connection occurs and the crime rate goes up.

Pocket parks and neighborhood green spaces foster a sense of shelter and security.

Crime and the fear of crime affects both victims and the community alike. In addition to the human cost, there is also an economic price, including property loss, medical care, and lost wages. The causes of crime are complex, but growing scientific evidence reveals that nature plays an important role in creating safe communal spaces that encourage neighbors to get to know one another.

Research reveals that urban residents dislike—even fear—treeless, empty common spaces. The addition of trees and other plantings dramatically changes their perception of those spaces. Outdoor spaces with green landscaping suffer less from graffiti, vandalism, and littering than comparable spaces without plantings. Hotter temperatures correlate with rises in assault, burglary, robbery, and theft. Not only do trees offer cooling shade and reduce the impact of urban heat islands, planting trees in open urban spaces also improves the physical environment and character of a community. Trees are a powerful factor in helping to reduce crime and create safe neighborhoods. What's more, collaborative planting projects strengthen trust and create an environment where people work together, building a close-knit community that is more resilient to crime.

WELCOME TO THE NEIGHBORHOOD

Community thrives in green environments. People who take pride in their neighborhoods feel a sense of belonging and are more likely to get along. They socialize and watch out for one another. This level of healthy social

↓ Neighborhood trees create a vibrant sense of community.

↑ Mature trees boost curb appeal and increase home values.

capital is the foundation of a strong community—and in its absence, neighborhoods suffer.

The simple act of planting trees helps improve local living conditions and boosts people's pride in their surroundings. Coming together to plant trees is a great way to build relationships while enriching the quality of life for everyone who lives in the community. Ultimately, greening a neighborhood, town, or city strengthens social bonds and bolsters pride, ensuring cultural vitality for generations to come.

BOOSTING PROPERTY VALUE

Owning a home is seen by many as part of the American dream. A house is an emotional center of family and a literal shelter from the outside world. Owning a home also builds financial security as it increases in value and

Partnering to Plant an Urban Canopy

MAYOR G. T. BYNUM

One of Tulsa's greatest conservation achievements has been the founding of Up With Trees, a non-profit organization dedicated to planting, preserving, and promoting the urban forest. In 1975, a high school student asked Tulsa Streets Commissioner Sid Patterson if the city was going to replace trees after removing them for a street widening project. Patterson then started Up With Trees with the full support of Mayor Robert LaFortune.

Since its inception, Up With Trees has planted more than 33,000 trees in public spaces within the city. These plantings have required ongoing collaboration and support of subsequent administrations, the Tulsa City Council, and numerous city departments. Although many city properties were planted over the first three decades, the most significant collaborations grew out of a natural disaster—the December 2007 ice storm.

After this devastating storm destroyed tens of thousands of Tulsa's trees, Mayor Kathy Taylor worked with Up With Trees on the ReGreen Tulsa initiative to plant 10,000 trees citywide—a goal that was achieved in 2015. This helped strengthen the relationships between Up With Trees and city departments, which still serve in the growth of Tulsa's urban forestry programs today.

Within Tulsa's city parks, Up With Trees has planted and tended more than 3000 trees. Tulsa

Parks and Up With Trees also host the annual Arbor Day celebration. This year, community volunteers, students, and urban forestry partners came together to commemorate Tulsa's recognition as a Tree City USA for 28 years running.

While working with the city's Streets and Stormwater Department, Up With Trees has been able to plant hundreds of trees around flood detention areas. Many of these areas double as recreational venues for soccer, football, and softball. The partnership with Streets and Stormwater also has allowed for the planting and establishment of more than 1000 trees along major arterial roadways and medians throughout Tulsa. Since 2012, Up With Trees has taken over the maintenance of forty-three city medians with more than 430 trees.

Most recently, Up With Trees worked with our Engineering Services Department to plant 1563 trees along highways between Tulsa International Airport and downtown. We invested $1.5 million from the Improve Our Tulsa capital funding program for this first phase of Up With Trees' Tulsa's Gateway to the World project.

Building on this established public–private partnership between the City of Tulsa and Up With Trees, our city continues to benefit from a healthier urban forest and enriched quality of life.

↑ Mature trees in an established neighborhood create a sense of home.

accrues equity. Real estate agents have long known that trees increase curb appeal and help boost sale prices. Studies have even shown that a home with more trees tends to have a higher value than one with fewer trees. Buyers are simply willing to pay more for real estate with a beautiful landscape and mature plantings. Of course, as trees mature, their impact and all the benefits we've discussed grow along with the size of their canopy. Without a doubt, planting and caring for trees pays economic dividends along with enhancing everyday life.

A CALL TO ACTION

Everybody loves trees, but sometimes it's easy to take them for granted. Take a walk around your neighborhood and list all the ways that trees are—or could be—providing benefits that support a good life and a healthy neighborhood. Think about the functional value of the trees in your community, how they provide shade and help to capture and slow the rain and reduce stormwater runoff. And, of course, think about how they lend beauty and value to your neighborhood and create inviting gathering places.

How can you help enhance and grow the tree canopy where you live? Encourage city planners to support public health by installing parks near where people live and work and converting underused properties and common spaces into green assets like parks, community gardens, or attractive stormwater management features.

CHAPTER 5

IT'S TIME TO PLANT

We've covered a lot of ground about the importance of trees and forests and the urgent need to promote their use as nature-based solutions to many of today's social and environmental challenges. Now it's time to start planning for and planting trees. ▶

↑ Put trees to work in your landscape.

This is your chance to engage in the tree planting movement and make a difference as you plant trees to create beauty around your home and enrich your neighborhood and surrounding community.

Planting trees is exciting. Imagine how your trees will look in your yard, the brilliant fall foliage and colorful spring blooms. When planting trees, you are quite literally laying down roots for a better future, and growing a legacy for generations to come. So, when you decide to plant, you want to get it right.

It is important to consider where you are planting, how you can put trees to work in your landscape, and, finally, what trees you will select. Thoughtful preparation will pay off by providing decades of enjoyment, beauty, and benefits.

The Arbor Day Foundation's website (arborday.org) has a comprehensive set of guides and extensive information about tree species, selection, planting, and care, including a zip code tool that makes it easy to find your hardiness zone. In chapters 5 and 6, you'll find the tried and true fundamentals to get you started planting trees in your landscape.

RIGHT TREE, RIGHT PLACE

In previous chapters, we examined how trees support a healthy climate, provide environmental benefits, strengthen community, and foster personal wellness. Now it's time to bring it all home and look at how you can put the power of trees to work in your neighborhood and home landscape.

GROWING REGIONS

The first thing to consider is where you are. Choosing a tree that will flourish in your growing region is fundamental to becoming a successful tree planter. Every region is filled with countless topographic variations and microclimates that influence local growing conditions. The growing regions listed here describe the attributes that distinguish one region from another and name the hardiness zones they encompass.

The NORTHWEST (NW) growing region encompasses coastal Northern California, western Oregon, western Washington, and up into southern British Columbia and southeastern Alaska. This growing region is characterized by mild, wet winters and not-too-hot, dry summers. Zones 7–8.

→ Red maple (*Acer rubrum*) trees flourish in much of the United States, including the Northwest region.

The **NORTH** (N) ranges from Saskatchewan and Alberta to the north, sweeping down through the Dakotas, Montana, Wyoming, Idaho, eastern Washington, eastern Oregon, and extending to Colorado, Utah, and Nevada. Each state or province has a multitude of growing conditions, but elevation and precipitation are the overriding factors for gardeners. Numerous mountain ranges dictate rapid increases in elevation, corresponding to a decrease in average temperatures. Precipitation can range from 30 inches or more on the western slopes of mountains, to just 10 to 15 inches on the drier plains to the east. Zones 3–7.

← Quaking aspen (*Populus tremuloides*) is native to cooler areas of North America.

The **SOUTHWEST** (SW) growing region is a land of year-round sunshine and warm weather, right? Well, yes and no. While sunshine is nearly constant throughout the year in Southern California, Arizona, New Mexico, and West Texas, local growing conditions are greatly influenced by elevation and precipitation patterns. But come summer it's all hot! Lack of rain is also a limiting factor in this predominantly dry region. Zones 4–10.

← Desert-willow (*Chilopsis linearis*) thrives in the arid Southwest.

The MIDWEST (MW) forms the geographic heart of the United States and Canada, where winters are typically cold and snowy and summers are hot and humid with intense thunderstorms. This sweeping growing region covers Manitoba, central and western Ontario, Nebraska, Kansas, Minnesota, Wisconsin, Michigan, Iowa, Missouri, Illinois, Indiana, and Ohio. Zones 3–7.

→ Bur oak (*Quercus macrocarpa*) trees are typically large and long-lived throughout the Midwest.

The SOUTHERN PLAINS (SP) is characterized by dramatic, diverse, and powerful weather throughout central, South, and East Texas and Oklahoma. Total annual rainfall varies widely across this region, from as little as 17 inches in the Oklahoma Panhandle to an average of 50 inches in Houston. Zones 6–9.

→ Crapemyrtle (*Lagerstroemia indica*) is often referred to as the "lilac of the South" and blooms reliably in the Southern Plains growing region.

The SOUTH (S) is warm and wet, with long hot summers with high humidity and mild winters. This region includes Kentucky, Tennessee, Arkansas, Louisiana, Mississippi, Alabama, North Florida, Georgia, South Carolina, and North Carolina. Zones 6–9.

← Southern magnolia (*Magnolia grandiflora*), with flowers that reach up to 6 inches across, is a popular ornamental tree in the South.

The MID-ATLANTIC (MA) region encompasses West Virginia, Virginia, Washington, D.C., Maryland, Delaware, New Jersey, and Pennsylvania. Snowfall typically blankets the ground for only a portion of the winter months, and summers are warm and humid. Rainfall patterns are generally moderate, but coastal storms can bring periodic heavy precipitation. Zones 5–7.

← Tulip poplar (*Liriodendron tulipifera*) is native to the Mid-Atlantic region.

The NORTHEAST (NE) is a diverse region whose climate is affected by mountains, valleys, a long coastline, and numerous rivers and lakes. This region includes Quebec, eastern Ontario, Maine, New Hampshire, Vermont, Massachusetts, New York, Rhode Island, and Connecticut. Winters are snowy, and summers are temperate and humid, with average precipitation of 40 inches or more and snowfall between 60 and 90 inches. Zones 3–7.

→ Eastern white pine (*Pinus strobus*), with its clusters of soft needles, is a hardy tree in several regions, including the Northeast.

The TROPICAL (TR) region includes South Florida, Puerto Rico, and the Virgin Islands. This region is characterized by rainy and dry seasons and hot, humid conditions much of the year. Temperatures regularly exceed 90°F, but ocean breezes offer comfortable outdoor conditions. Rainfall is seasonal and plentiful, especially during hurricane season. Zone 10 and warmer.

→ Sweet acacia (*Vachellia farnesiana*), with very fragrant globe-shaped flowerheads, is native to tropical regions of the Americas.

WHAT ARE HARDINESS ZONES?

Hardiness is a plant's ability to survive in the extreme temperatures of the particular geographic region in which you are planting. Plants can be cold hardy, heat tolerant, or both.

The U.S. Department of Agriculture's Plant Hardiness Zone Map divides the United States and Canada into eleven areas determined by average minimum winter temperatures and is the industry standard for most garden books and plant labels. For instance, if a tree is said to be hardy to zone 4, that means that it can be expected withstand a minimum temperature of −30° to −40°F. The system is a general guide for selecting plants suitable for your growing region.

However, a site's microclimate—representing local conditions such as soil properties, light intensity, proximity to a body of water, prevailing winds, and even distance from a heat-reflective wall—affects the actual growing conditions in your garden. And, as an added consideration, urban areas tend to be warmer than suburban and rural environments due to the urban heat island effect.

PLAN AND PLANT FOR SUCCESS

The best way to encourage healthy, strong growth and minimize complications from pests and disease is to select a tree that is a good match for the growing conditions offered by your planting site. According to the International Society of Arboriculture, planting a tree ill-suited to a site is the number one cause of failure—even more than insect- and disease-related tree deaths.

To get your tree off to a strong start and a long life, familiarize yourself with the growing conditions of your planting site. Then take a look around at established trees that are already thriving in your immediate neighborhood. This is valuable information you can use when deciding what tree

→ Trees add value to the home landscape.

Plan and prepare for tree planting success.

↑ Mature trees line a neighborhood street.

to plant on your property. The beautiful, mature specimen trees you see in historic neighborhoods and in landscape photography would never have reached their full potential if they were planted in improperly matched sites.

EXPOSURE

Most trees require full sunlight for proper growth and flowering. Some do well in (or even prefer) partial or light shade, but few tree species perform well in dense shade. The amount of available sunlight at your planting location will determine which tree species will be successful. Yet navigating various degrees of sun and shade referenced on plant labels can be confusing. The following guidelines may help.

Full sun Six hours or more of direct sunlight per day. This doesn't have to be continuous sun—you might get 3 hours in the morning before the sun goes behind a tree or building and then another 4 hours later in the afternoon.

Partial shade It's a nuance call. A location that receives partial sun may get less than the 6 hours a day necessary to be considered full sun, or it may get only broken light, dappled through an overhead tree canopy. Many understory trees do well in these conditions.

Wind exposure is also a factor to consider when assessing your planting site. Wind can dry out soils, damage tree crowns, and uproot newly planted trees. Special maintenance, such as staking or more frequent watering, may be necessary to establish young trees on windy sites.

SOIL

Next it's time to evaluate what's happening underground. Healthy soil contains a mix of organic matter, minerals, air spaces, and living microbes. Collectively, these components are responsible for creating soil structure and determine fertility. For your tree to thrive, it's important choose a tree species that will remain healthy and reach maturity in the soil you plant it in.

Before you embark on a large-scale planting scheme or plant expensive specimen trees, getting your soil tested by a professional lab is a modest investment and a smart move. Consult an arborist, your local independent

↓ Healthy soil is living soil.

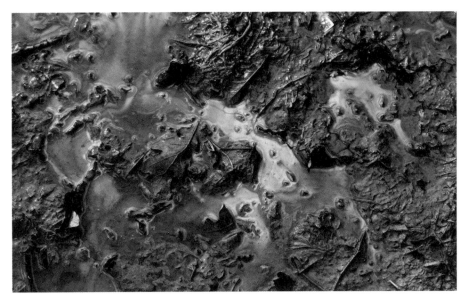

↑ Most trees will not tolerate poor drainage conditions.

nursery, or research local soil labs online for instructions on how to collect soil samples and where to send them for analysis. Test results, which usually arrive in a couple of weeks, provide a complete analysis of nutrients, possible contamination, and pH (alkalinity or acidity) and offer specific directions for correcting any revealed deficiencies.

If you're landscaping around new construction or in a dense urban area, where soil is often disturbed, shallow, and compacted, it's critical that you address and correct drainage problems before planting. Pooling water or mucky clay soil limits the availability of oxygen, which roots need, and may ultimately kill the tree. Consult a professional landscaper or arborist for advice if you suspect drainage problems.

Before you dig, call 811 or make an online request a few days before you plan to plant. Local authorities will reach out to utility operators who, if necessary, will come out to mark or flag any buried utility lines on your property.

AVAILABLE SPACE

Overhead or underground utilities, pavement, buildings, other trees, traffic intersections, and many other factors determine or limit the planting space in the built environment. The list goes on and on. Selecting the right tree for your available space is the first step toward assuring your tree will grow to maturity and contribute to your landscape for years to come.

Once you have a sense of how much planting space is available, you can select a tree with the appropriate growth habit and form that will be a good fit for the site. All young trees are attractive, but it's important to

↓ Plant the right tree in the right place, taking care to place taller trees well away from overhead utility lines.

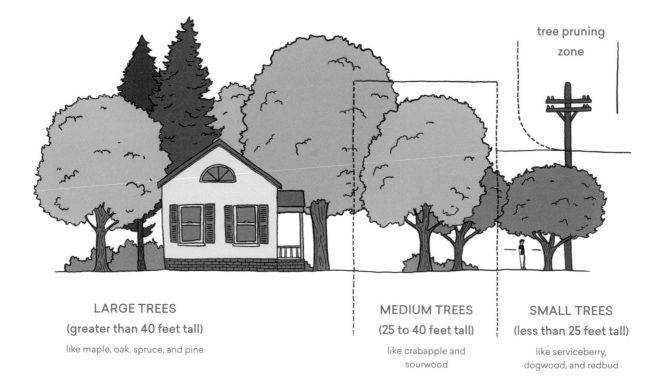

tree pruning zone

LARGE TREES
(greater than 40 feet tall)
like maple, oak, spruce, and pine

MEDIUM TREES
(25 to 40 feet tall)
like crabapple and sourwood

SMALL TREES
(less than 25 feet tall)
like serviceberry, dogwood, and redbud

→ When planting a young tree near a utility line, it is important to consider the ill effects of necessary utility pruning of the mature tree.

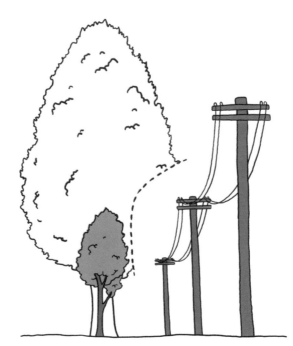

RIGHT TREE, RIGHT PLACE

117

factor in anticipated height and crown spread *at maturity*. When possible, avoid planting beneath or near utility lines, as this is the safer option and ensures a long life for your tree. When planting beneath utility lines, select trees that will mature at a small stature to avoid unnecessary and potentially harmful pruning.

How long will it take for your tree to reach its full height? Some tree species grow much faster than others, which is great if you're looking for a quick privacy screen. However, slow-growing species typically live longer than those with a faster growth habit. Local growing conditions dramatically affect growth, so more often than not rates are described in relative terms as fast, medium, or slow. Check with your local arborist or nursery professional for expected performance in your region.

The crown of a tree, made up of the leaves and the branches, determines the form or the shape of a tree's canopy. A columnar tree will require less space. Round, oval, vase-shaped, and pyramidal trees have a much broader crown and therefore provide the most shade.

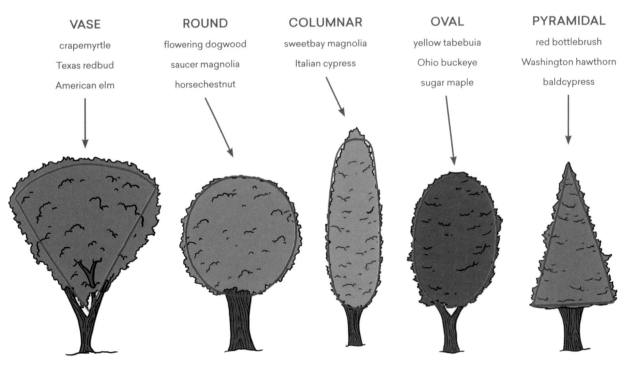

VASE
crapemyrtle
Texas redbud
American elm

ROUND
flowering dogwood
saucer magnolia
horsechestnut

COLUMNAR
sweetbay magnolia
Italian cypress

OVAL
yellow tabebuia
Ohio buckeye
sugar maple

PYRAMIDAL
red bottlebrush
Washington hawthorn
baldcypress

↑ Get familiar with the variety of tree growth habits to select the best shape for your planting location.

↑ Healthy trees beautify the landscape.

PLANTING WITH PURPOSE

Practically speaking, when trees are strategically placed they can conserve energy. Using trees to cool things down in summer and help conserve warmth in winter results in energy savings for you, while also lessening the toll on local utilities. This translates into a reduction in fossil fuel consumption used by utilities to create energy, which means less carbon dioxide emissions. You can make a difference. Every tree planted puts us one step closer to a cooler planet.

Life is better with trees. Healthy trees beautify your landscape and create pleasant, livable spaces. They can also increase the value of your property. Many trees have the potential to outlive the person who planted them, so getting things right today will have a positive impact on your landscape for years to come. Before you get too specific about which tree to plant, take the time to think about all of the powerful and purposeful ways that trees can contribute to your property and support your community canopy.

What you want a tree to provide may include moderating the temperature in your home, increasing privacy, reducing street noise, or improving your property's curb appeal. It's all information you should consider before moving on to selecting a particular species for your landscape.

BEAT THE HEAT

Trees in the landscape can lower temperatures on your property in a number of ways. Cool shade physically blocks or diminishes the sun's radiant heat, offering welcome relief on a hot summer day. A shaded play area protects delicate skin from burning rays. A mature tree canopy also tempers heat by elevating the ambient humidity. Think of it as a cooling exhale—you'll never get that from a patio umbrella.

Plant a deciduous tree near the southwestern corner of your home to provide cooling. Of course, the size and spread of the mature tree will determine the amount of shade cast on windows and roofs. Here's a simple calculation to help you envision future benefits: A tree will cast a shadow roughly equal to its height during the latter part of the afternoon in summer.

↓ Trees can be strategically placed to cool your property in summer.

Site a tree near a home's southwestern corner to provide afternoon shade in summer.

Shade pavement to reduce the heat.

Medium and small trees are often the best choice for the scale of many inner city lots. Medium-sized trees, such as a distinctive crabapple with a rounded form and medium growth habit, can be planted 15 to 20 feet from the house. Small trees, such as a flowering dogwood, may be planted as close as 10 feet away. Large trees, like the northern red oak, can quickly grow to 60 to 75 feet tall by 45 feet wide and should be sited 20 feet or more away from the house.

Ideally, align trees to shade windows but prune lower branches to prevent blocking views, especially if your shade tree is located in the front yard. You can also plant a tree to shade an air conditioner to keep it cool and running more efficiently. Shading patios, sidewalks, and the driveway cools the pavement, the entire yard, and even brings down the temperature of the neighborhood.

WARMTH IN WINTER

On the flip side of the calendar, the bare branches of deciduous trees in winter allow sunshine to warm your home and flood interior spaces with

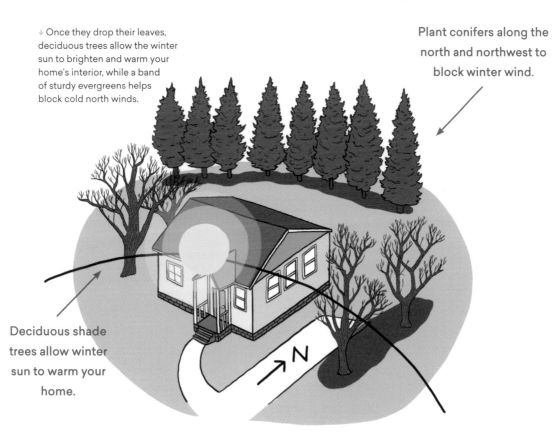

↓ Once they drop their leaves, deciduous trees allow the winter sun to brighten and warm your home's interior, while a band of sturdy evergreens helps block cold north winds.

Plant conifers along the north and northwest to block winter wind.

Deciduous shade trees allow winter sun to warm your home.

↑ Evergreen trees can provide a windbreak in winter.

much needed light. The sun's path in the sky is lower on the horizon in winter, so you'll want to avoid planting evergreen trees on the southern side of your home, where they would block winter sunshine and may result in an increase in heating costs.

Planting a row of dense evergreens on the northern and northwestern sides of your property creates a windbreak against cold winter winds, reducing heat loss through windows and minimizing chilly drafts. The downwind, or sheltered, side of a tree or line of trees is where the most snow accumulates, so plant your windbreak at a distance of one or two tree heights from your rooftop and driveway, if you have the space.

I-TREE MY TREE

The My Tree calculator is a simple and accessible online tool powered by i-Tree, a peer-reviewed software suite developed by tree care professionals in collaboration with government and private organizations including the USDA Forest Service and Davey Tree. Simply enter your location and provide details about your tree species and size. The calculator then serves up compelling information that will help you understand the environmental value your tree provides on an annual basis and how projected benefits can be expected to grow with time.

For instance, say you have a relatively young flowering cherry in your Seattle landscape with a trunk diameter of 5 inches. The calculator estimates your tree will intercept 623 gallons of rainfall and reduce atmospheric carbon by 82 pounds annually.

Or say you live in Adair, Iowa, where you have an Ohio buckeye that is 10 inches in diameter. The calculator estimates that your buckeye will intercept 1160 gallons of rainfall and remove 538 pounds of atmospheric carbon each year.

Suppose you live in the desert Southwest where the sun shines all year and you're lucky enough to have a fairly mature honeylocust with a trunk that's 15 inches in diameter. This year your honeylocust will intercept 1013 gallons of rainfall and remove 18 pounds of atmospheric carbon. However, as you care for your honeylocust and the trunk grows to 20 inches in diameter, the annual rainfall intercepted will increase to 1430 gallons, while the carbon sequestered declines a bit to 11 pounds as the tree loses branches and begins to decay with age.

NEIGHBORLY TREES

A verdant canopy creates a sense of sanctuary and seclusion from the outside world—just ask any child who is lucky enough to have a tree house. Especially in towns where houses are spaced close together, a leafy screen can block unwanted views and shelter windows from prying eyes or the glare of passing car lights. Or maybe you'd just rather not look out at the driveway. Planting a Japanese maple with a graceful fan shape and multiple seasons of interest won't actually block an unfortunate view, but it can interrupt sight lines and focus attention on the intermediate space, effectively distracting from what lies beyond it.

A solid fence around your property says "Keep out!" in no uncertain terms, whereas a living fence offers a more friendly face to the outside world. A row of tidy evergreens planted along a property line helps keep children and pets in the yard, while buffering noise and filtering irritants, like dust, pollen, and street-level particulates, which in turn reduces indoor air pollution.

When things get loud, a well-placed hedge can also absorb and deflect sound. Evergreen trees with foliage that extends all the way to the ground— such as arborvitae or Leyland cypress if you've got the space—provide a year-round buffer for street noise. To a lesser degree, deciduous trees are also effective but only during that part of the year when they have leaves.

You can also plant trees to form an interior screen on your property to create a garden room within the larger landscape, define the vegetable garden, or deflect attention from a utilitarian outdoor space like a tool shed or garbage cans. In fact, if you've got the planting space and can accommodate clearances, trees can become a dynamic, living softscape. Just be sure to be considerate and avoid planting trees where storm-tossed branches might fall on your neighbor's property.

STREET TREES

Whether it's a stately boulevard lined with trees or a shady side street, trees enhance the quality of life in a community. Street trees help create a sense of neighborhood identity and improve living conditions by shading overheated pavement, filtering pollutants, reducing storm runoff, and pumping oxygen into the air we breathe.

Trees planted in the narrow median of space that falls between the sidewalk and the curb play an important role in creating community canopy. They also face specific challenges, however, including toxic roadway

↑ Situate trees and shrubs to screen unwanted views.

↓ Be a good citizen and consider how trees will impact neighbors.

↑ Trees provide a buffer from street noise and light.

When planting street trees, be sure to factor in available planting space, roadway and pedestrian clearances, and overhead utilities.

emissions, limited growing space, and compacted soil. The best street trees are hardy, tough, and resilient. And for safety reasons, their growth habit and branching structure must accommodate limitations imposed by sidewalks, driveways, streetlights, power poles, and overhead wires.

Street-side planting space is typically public property. Before planting, check with your local municipality to discover rules, restrictions, and possible permit requirements. Fortunately, a growing number of cities recognize the importance of investing in a healthy urban forest and provide valuable resources for homeowners, like a list of recommended trees that will thrive in your growing region, planting instructions and advice on caring for young trees, and information about how to be a good steward of mature trees. Some even offer financial assistance or free trees!

Here are some tips for selecting a good street tree:

- When planting a tree beneath overhead wires, choose a tree with a *mature* height of no more than 25 feet.

- Situate trees to avoid blocking streetlights, for safety reasons.

- Avoid planting trees that tend to damage nearby infrastructure as they age. Tree roots can invade cracked or broken water and sewage connections, requiring costly repairs, or lift up sidewalks to pose a tripping hazard.

- Consider how a tree's branches might interfere with drivers' sight lines and people passing by on the sidewalk or getting in or out of cars. Leave lower branches on newly planted young trees, which will help increase their trunk diameter. But once the tree is established, remove the lowest branches to allow clear passage and sight lines.

CHOOSING YOUR TREES

Finally, we arrive at the marvelous dilemma of choosing which tree you will plant on your property. A beautiful tree becomes a focal point. The play of shifting light and shadow animates the landscape. Flowers, fruit, and shelter attract birds and other wildlife. And as the trunk grows and the canopy expands, your tree will become a record of time, a member of the family.

Trees are both purposeful and pleasing, a striking design element that creates interest and invites engagement with the natural world throughout the entire year. While it's true that a row of columnar American arborvitae

Making Memories with Family Trees

RYAN NEWMAN, NASCAR driver

I've been driving NASCAR stock cars for over 20 years, and I love my job. Unfortunately, it isn't environmentally friendly, so I work hard to improve our environment in many other ways. Over the years, I've worked on various projects with the Arbor Day Foundation as well as with racetracks to install solar power stations.

You'll read about all kinds of environmental concerns within the pages of this book. These threats are legit. But one of the simplest (and best) ways to offset the damage done to the environment is to plant trees. Trees hold onto carbon, keeping it locked in their roots rather than escaping into the atmosphere and warming our world. That is a fact. But trees also give us shade, food in the form of fruits and nuts, and lumber, not to mention beauty. Trees provide habitats for you and me, and so many living creatures in our world.

I grew up in South Bend, Indiana, on a rural tract of 5 acres that included a fruit orchard. Today, I have a 200-acre farm with black angus cows, a small herd of buffalo, ponds, and a managed white-tailed deer population. Thinking back to my childhood home, I decided to add an orchard to my farm, but this time with more purpose. I personally planted more than 75 apple, pear, peach, and pawpaw trees with the goal of providing habitat and food for my family and the animals.

I love the outdoors and share that love with my two daughters. My youngest daughter, Ashlyn, loves acorns. If you ask her what her favorite tree is, she will tell you "It's an oak." As I travel across the country racing, I bring back different species of acorns from different geographic areas. Yes, I know they won't all grow in our zone, but that doesn't stop us from planting them. It's a great way to learn about nature while passing on my love for trees to my children.

Last July, my oldest daughter, Brooklyn, decided to give her sister Ashlyn a treehouse for her eighth birthday. Together we picked a spot on the farm with two giant mature white oaks. We used cedar trees that were downed in a storm for the stairs and handrails and even found a 15-foot cedar that was dead and still standing to use as a chase for the power and water to get up to the treehouse. Knowing that the girls were an integral part of every decision in building the treehouse makes it a very special project for a very proud father.

Just one more priceless thing that trees provide—memories.

↑ Planting trees in a variety of sizes, forms, and seasonal displays adds interest to your landscape throughout the year.

← It's best to know what you want in a tree before going to the nursery.

will provide privacy and buffer noise, its highest calling may be to provide an emerald backdrop for the early spring blossoms of a flowering cherry, crabapple, or saucer magnolia. Plant some shade-loving hostas under your flowering trees and suddenly you have a whole new look, with layers of green on green that will last all summer. As temperatures drop and deciduous foliage changes color, your landscape is transformed once again without lifting a shovel. Finally, those leaves drop to reveal the structural form of the trees' trunks and bare branches against the evergreen backdrop in winter, with bonus design and wildlife points for persistent fruit during dormancy.

Consider interior views as well. A prominent window that looks out on an ornamental tree allows you to revel in seasonal blossoms or watch cavorting birds as they feast on fall fruit from the comfort of indoors. Trees in the landscape are constant companions in every season.

↑ Pink flowers appear along the stems of eastern redbud (*Cercis canadensis*) in spring.

FLOWERING TREES

Welcome spring or liven up the dog days of summer with color, birdsong, and possibly fruit by planting one of these popular flowering trees.

DESERT-WILLOW (*Chilopsis linearis*) is a small, multi-trunked tree native to the desert Southwest that prefers full sun and is extremely drought tolerant. The tree bears narrow leaves and showy blooms in summer. The well-branched growth habit and density make the desert-willow well suited for a wide screen or tall hedge. It has a vase-shaped form with medium growth to 15 to 25 feet tall by 10 feet wide. Zones 7–9.

← EASTERN REDBUD (*Cercis canadensis*) makes a bold landscape statement with a spreading, graceful form. Profuse delicate rosy, pink flowers appear along the stems in April, providing one of the season's most dramatic displays. Heart-shaped leaves emerge reddish purple before changing to dark green in summer, with handsome golden fall foliage. Eastern redbud has a rounded canopy with medium growth to 20 to 30 feet tall by 25 to 35 feet wide. Zones 4–9.

FLOWERING DOGWOOD (*Cornus florida*) is an excellent landscape choice for all four seasons. Showy white bracts appear in spring, foliage turns a vibrant red purple in fall, and glossy red fruits attract winter songbirds to the enjoyment of all. This tree offers nice contrast when planted along with pink or red dogwoods with larger evergreens in the background. Flowering dogwood has a rounded canopy with medium growth to 20 to 25 feet tall and as wide. Zones 5–9.

SAUCER MAGNOLIA (*Magnolia ×soulangeana*) is a showstopper in the landscape. Numerous large goblets of fragrant pink and white flowers appear in early spring. After blooming, broad, dark green leaves clothe the small, low-branched tree, contrasting with the smooth silvery gray bark. Saucer magnolia has a rounded canopy with medium growth to 20 to 30 feet tall and as wide. Zones 4–9.

YOSHINO CHERRY (*Prunus ×yedoensis*), also known as the Japanese flowering cherry, is the darling of the flowering tree world. It's famous for its vibrant display of pink and white blossoms and faint almond fragrance in the springtime. In the summer, this tree will be a highlight in the yard, with its elegant branching pattern, glossy bark, and dark green leaves. Yoshino cherry has a rounded canopy with medium growth to 30 to 40 feet tall by 25 to 40 feet wide. Zones 5–8.

FABULOUS FORM

Landscaping with trees is an opportunity to introduce striking personality and year-round interest to your property. From strong evergreen silhouettes to interesting bark and seasonal foliage, these trees deliver.

AMERICAN SWEETGUM (*Liquidambar styraciflua*) is an attractive shade tree with glossy star-shaped leaves, good fall color that persists late into the season, interesting fruit, and twigs with unique corky growths called wings. Native to North America, mature trees are prized specimen in parks, campuses, and large yards across the country. American sweetgum has an oval canopy with medium to fast growth up to 75 feet tall by 40 to 50 feet wide. Zones 5–9.

→ ATLAS CEDAR (*Cedrus atlantica*), with distinctive silvery blue to bluish green evergreen needles, makes a strikingly beautiful specimen in the landscape. When given the time and the space to grow freely, Atlas cedar develops an attractive rugged form in maturity. The tree has a pyramidal form with slow growth to 40 to 60 feet tall by 30 to 40 feet wide. Zones 6–9.

GINKGO (*Ginkgo biloba*) is living history, with earliest leaf fossils dating from 270 million years ago. It is one of the most distinct and beautiful of all deciduous trees, with unique fan-shaped leaves that turn a stunning yellow in the fall. Ginkgo establishes easily and can tolerate many urban conditions, including heat, air pollution, salt, and confined spaces. It has a pyramidal form with medium growth to 25 to 50 feet tall by 25 to 35 feet wide. Zones 3–8.

KENTUCKY COFFEETREE (*Gymnocladus dioicus*) is an excellent choice for parks, golf courses, and other large areas. Tolerant of both pollution and drought, this tough species is also widely used as an ornamental in the home landscape or as a resilient street tree. Kentucky coffeetree has an oval canopy with slow to medium growth to 60 to 75 feet tall by 40 to 50 feet wide. Zones 3–8.

RIVER BIRCH (*Betula nigra*) grows naturally along riverbanks, but as a landscape tree it can be planted almost anywhere in the United States. The species is valued for its unique cinnamon-colored bark that curls and peels at maturity and brilliant yellow fall color. River birch has an oval canopy with fast growth to 40 to 70 feet tall by 40 to 60 feet wide. Zones 4–9.

SOURWOOD (*Oxydendrum arboreum*) shines in the landscape as a specimen in a lawn, a garden feature, an ornamental addition to larger trees, or

↑ Atlas cedar (*Cedrus atlantica*) produces an abundance of silvery blue needles.

when planted in a clump in a large open space. Fragrant, drooping flowers that resemble lily-of-the-valley appear in midsummer against the lustrous green foliage. Leaves turn intensely beautiful shades of brilliant crimson, purplish red, and sometimes yellow in fall. Sourwood has an oval canopy with medium growth to 25 to 30 feet tall by 20 feet wide. Zones 5–9.

↑ The radiant red leaves of *Acer rubrum* 'October Glory' last for several weeks.

When you plant a fast-growing tree, you'll realize the benefits of a mature tree sooner. So, whether you're dreaming of cool green shade or looking to establish privacy, the following trees will get you there quickly.

EASTERN WHITE PINE (*Pinus strobus*) is a hardy, valuable tree with clusters of long, slender blue-green needles that are soft and flexible and elongated, slightly curved brown cones that grow 3 to 8 inches long. This evergreen is striking in the winter landscape, where it makes an ideal windbreak. Eastern white pine has an oval form with fast growth to 50 to 80 feet tall by 20 to 40 feet wide. Zones 3–8.

← OCTOBER GLORY RED MAPLE (*Acer rubrum* 'October Glory') is a popular and beautiful shade tree. Glistening dark green leaves in spring and summer turn radiant red in late fall and persist for several weeks. Showy red fruit attracts many birds and other wildlife. This cultivar has an oval canopy with medium to fast growth to 40 to 50 feet tall by 25 to 30 feet wide. Zones 3–9.

PAPER BIRCH (*Betula papyrifera*) is one of the best-loved trees of the New England landscape, frequently planted for the beauty of its distinctive smooth white bark that curls and peels with maturity. Its dark green leaves turn brilliant gold in fall, a signature spectacle of many northern forests. Paper birch has an oval canopy with medium to fast growth to 50 to 70 feet tall by 35 feet wide. Zones 2–7.

PIN OAK (*Quercus palustris*) is a large shade tree that quickly reaches its mature height, growing about 2.5 feet per year on average. Glossy dark green leaves turn russet, bronze, or red in fall. The tree's form is pyramidal through early maturity but becomes more oval with age, with fast growth to 60 to 70 feet tall by 25 to 45 feet wide. Zones 4–8.

QUAKING ASPEN (*Populus tremuloides*) has the widest natural range of any tree in North America and a clonal growth habit that spreads by sending up multiple shoots from a single root system. Its rounded, triangular green leaves flutter (or quake) in the slightest breeze; they turn deep yellow in fall and contrast with the smooth, greenish white bark. Quaking aspen has an oval canopy with fast growth to 40 to 50 feet tall by 20 to 30 feet wide. Zones 1–7.

STATURE AND SHADE

If you have the space, it's time to think big. Plant a family-friendly shade tree to mark the birth of a child or to celebrate the formation of a new family and establish a lasting legacy that endures from one generation to the next.

→ AMERICAN BEECH (*Fagus grandifolia*) is a beautiful native tree that holds a special place in many hearts. Formal and stately, in maturity the wide-spreading canopy provides expansive shade in the summer and offers beautiful bronze foliage in the fall. Birds, chipmunks, and squirrels forage the hard, brown beechnuts. American beech has an oval canopy with slow growth to 50 to 70 feet tall by 40 feet wide. Zones 4–9.

LACEBARK ELM (*Ulmus parvifolia*) is a handsome, graceful shade tree with a rounded spreading crown of lustrous dark green leaves and distinctive mottled bark that creates colorful patterns on the trunk. Fall foliage is yellow and reddish purple. It has a vase-shaped form with medium to fast growth to 40 to 50 feet tall by 35 to 45 feet wide. Zones 5–9.

NORTHERN CATALPA (*Catalpa speciosa*) demands attention with giant heart-shaped leaves and showy white flowers followed by dangling bean-like seed pods. A unique and hardy tree, northern catalpa is a fast grower well suited to large open spaces and parks. It has an oval canopy with fast growth to 40 to 60 feet tall by 20 to 40 feet wide. Zones 4–8.

NORTHERN RED OAK (*Quercus rubra*) is widely considered a national treasure. Naturalist Joseph S. Illick called the northern red oak "one of the handsomest, cleanest, and stateliest trees in North America." Versatile and hardy, it makes a good street tree with brilliant fall color and tolerates pollution and compacted soil. Northern red oak has a rounded canopy with fast growth to 60 to 75 feet tall by 45 feet wide. Zones 3–8.

SUGAR MAPLE (*Acer saccharum*) is a landscape standout and one of America's most-loved trees. In fact, more states have claimed it as their state tree than any other species. Medium to dark green leaves turn yellow, burnt orange, or red in fall. It is an excellent long-lived shade tree for planting where space allows. Sugar maple has an oval canopy with slow to medium growth to 60 to 75 feet tall by 40 to 50 feet wide. Zones 3–8.

THORNLESS HONEYLOCUST (*Gleditsia triacanthos* var. *inermis*) is a fast-growing tree with fragrant spring flowers and a delicate, open silhouette

↑ American beech (*Fagus grandifolia*) is a shade-tolerant tree with large, toothed leaves.

that lets grass grow underneath. Its fine-textured green leaflets turn clear yellow or yellow-green in fall and drop early. Honeylocust adapts to a wide range of soils and tolerates pollution, salt, and drought. It has an oval canopy with fast growth to 30 to 70 feet tall by 50 feet wide. Zones 3–9.

Serviceberry
(*Amelanchier*
canadensis)
offers plump
edible fruits
in summer.

WELCOME WILDLIFE

The following trees will enliven your landscape with wildlife and birdsong by providing shelter and food for birds and insects.

PURPLELEAF SAND CHERRY (*Prunus ×cistena*) is a very hardy small landscape tree with pale pink flowers in spring and reddish purple foliage that keeps its unique color all summer, offering good contrast with other plantings in a mixed hedge or beneath utility wires. Small sour cherries ripen in fall and furnish an important food source for birds and small mammals, while the density of its branches provides protection for nesting. Purpleleaf sand cherry has a rounded canopy with medium to fast growth to 7 to 10 feet tall by 5 to 7 feet wide. Zones 3-7.

PRAIRIFIRE FLOWERING CRABAPPLE (*Malus* 'Prairifire') is a showy disease-resistant tree that offers year-round beauty in the landscape. Dark red buds open to reddish pink flowers in spring with glossy reddish maroon leaves. Its foliage turns dark green in summer and a beautiful bronze color in fall, when small decorative purple fruits attract wildlife. The tree has a rounded canopy with medium growth to 15 to 20 feet tall by 15 to 20 feet wide. Zones 3-8.

← SERVICEBERRY (*Amelanchier canadensis*) is an all-season beauty native to eastern North American from Newfoundland south to Alabama. The tree bears beautiful white clusters of blooms early in the spring, followed by fresh green leaves that turn vibrant red and gold in the fall. Plump dark purple fruits that ripen in summer are favored by birds and humans alike. Serviceberry has a rounded canopy with medium growth to 15 to 25 feet tall by 15 to 25 feet wide. Zones 4-8.

SWEETBAY MAGNOLIA (*Magnolia virginiana*) has glistening dark green leaves with a silver underside that has a frosted appearance. The creamy 2- to 3-inch white flowers borne in late spring and early summer have a light lemon scent. Sweetbay magnolia is a lovely small patio or specimen tree with an elegant form. Its bright scarlet-red seeded fruit ripens in late summer, attracting many birds. The tree has a columnar form with medium growth to 10 to 20 feet tall and as wide. Zones 5-9.

WASHINGTON HAWTHORN (*Crataegus phaenopyrum*) is a medium tree. Its reddish purple leaves emerge in spring and turn dark green alongside a graceful display of white flowers. In autumn, the foliage turns orange, scarlet, or purple. Red berries extend the colorful show into winter. Washington hawthorn has a pyramidal canopy with medium growth to 25 to 30 feet tall by 20 to 25 feet wide. Zones 4-8.

The following ornamental fruit and nut trees will provide a beautiful and productive harvest along with delicate blooms and summer shade.

→ Oriental persimmon (*Diospyros kaki*) fruits are firm and have a mild sweet flavor.

FIG (*Ficus carica* 'Brown Turkey') is a handsome, multi-stemmed small tree with a striking silhouette and large deeply lobed green leaves. The tree produces two crops of sweet, brownish purple figs with an amber-colored, fine-grained flesh. The first (or breba) crop develops in spring on the previous year's growth. The main crop forms on the current season's growth and ripens in late summer or fall. Brown Turkey fig has a rounded canopy with medium growth to 10 to 20 feet tall by 12 to 15 feet wide. Zone 7-9.

LOQUAT (*Eriobotrya japonica*) is a small evergreen tree with lustrous large dark green leaves. Fragrant white flowers appear in fall, followed by sweet edible fruit where the climate is warm enough to ripen them. Loquat has a rounded canopy with fast growth to 15 to 25 feet tall and as wide. Zones 8-10.

→ ORIENTAL PERSIMMON (*Diospyros kaki*) is productive and has stunning fall foliage in shades of gold and red. The Fuyugaki persimmon, one of the most popular persimmon trees, produces 3- to 4-inch fruit in late fall. The fruit has a flavor that is non-astringent, mild, and sweet. The fruit has a firm texture and is great for fresh eating, pies, and jellies. The tree is self-fertile, pest and disease resistant, and drought tolerant. Oriental persimmon has an oval canopy with medium growth to 20 to 30 feet tall and as wide. Zones 7-10.

PAWPAW (*Asimina triloba*) is a North American native that will add a tropical vibe to your backyard, with large drooping leaves and unique purple flowers in April and May. In fall, oblong edible fruit that tastes like a mix of bananas, pineapples, and mangos ripens from yellow-green to dark brown. Two trees are required for pollination and fruit set. Pawpaw has a rounded canopy with medium growth to 15 to 25 feet tall and as wide. Zones 5-9.

PECAN (*Carya illinoinensis*), with a massive trunk and a spreading crown, is a fine ornamental tree in the landscape. The tree will produce a crop of sweet nuts, provided you plant more than one tree for pollination. Pecan has an oval canopy with medium growth to 70 to 100 feet tall by 55 feet wide. Zones 6-9.

A CALL TO ACTION

Now it's time to plant trees to make a difference! Complete the following questionnaire to guide your decision-making process and set you on the path to success.

Why is this tree being planted?

- ☐ Enhance existing landscape
- ☐ Part of a new landscape
- ☐ Wildlife support
- ☐ Commemorate a special occasion

What function will it serve?

- ☐ Design focal point
- ☐ Shade
- ☐ Privacy and buffer noise
- ☐ Edible fruits or nuts

What size tree is best suited for the location given the available space?

- ☐ Small tree (less than 25 feet tall)
- ☐ Medium tree (25 to 40 feet tall)
- ☐ Large tree (greater than 40 feet tall)

Have you considered practical clearances?

- ☐ Overhead utility lines
- ☐ Underground wiring and sewer or septic system
- ☐ Nearby sidewalks, patios, or driveways

Have you made a plan for the care and tending of your new tree?

- ☐ Will you be responsible for watering and tending your tree, or will you hire a tree service?
- ☐ Do you have the skills to prune a young tree, or will you hire an arborist?
- ☐ Are you prepared to do seasonal chores, like raking leaves and renewing mulch?

CHAPTER 6

A TREE PLANTER'S GUIDE TO TREES

Planting trees is inclusive and universal. It doesn't matter who you are, how old you are, or where you live— you can become a tree planter. If you're going to invest the energy and effort in planting trees, however, it's worth taking the time to get it right. ▶

In this chapter, we introduce some tree fundamentals. We'll help you select and plant a healthy tree and provide guidelines for getting your tree off to a good start and nurturing it in the years to come. Getting your tree well established is the best way to ensure future benefits and the promise of enjoying a beautiful long-lived tree.

TREES 101

We've learned a lot about how trees benefit us, our families, our communities, and even the planet. As in any good long-term relationship, though, it's also vital to learn about the inner workings of your partner in this relationship.

So, first, let's take a closer look at the anatomy of a tree.

- The CROWN of a tree, made up of the leaves and branches, primarily determines the form or shape of a tree's canopy.

- The main upright stem at the top of the trunk is the LEADER.

- BRANCHES divide from a tree's main trunk to provide a scaffold that supports and distributes leaves, flowers, and fruit efficiently.

- LEAVES use light and chlorophyll, the green pigment in plants, to convert energy from the sun into sugars that feed the tree, a process called photosynthesis. As byproducts of this process, leaves release oxygen and moisture into the atmosphere.

- The TRUNK of a tree provides support for the branches and the crown and serves as the main conduit for water from the soil and sugar from the leaves. The root collar (or trunk flare) is where the trunk expands at the base of the tree and connects to the roots.

- Tree ROOTS absorb water, minerals, and nutrients from the soil, anchor the tree to the ground, and store food reserves for the winter.

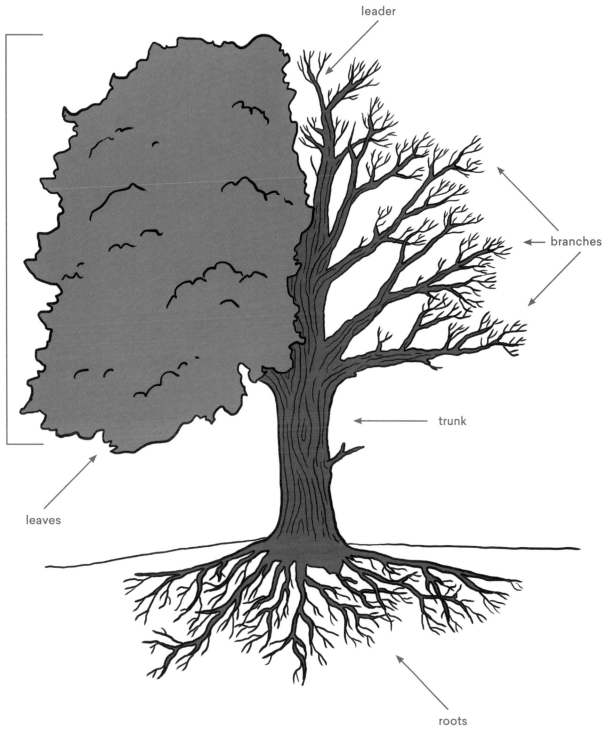

crown

leader

branches

trunk

leaves

roots

↑ The anatomy of a tree

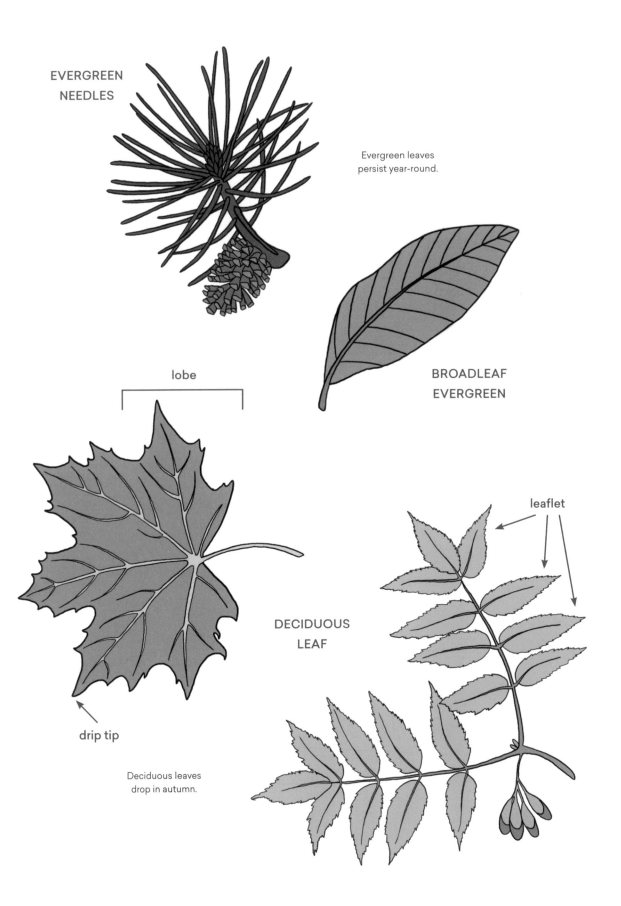

EVERGREEN
NEEDLES

Evergreen leaves
persist year-round.

BROADLEAF
EVERGREEN

lobe

drip tip

DECIDUOUS
LEAF

leaflet

Deciduous leaves
drop in autumn.

LEAVES

The nature and shape of a leaf contributes to how it serves the tree. Narrow evergreen needles expose a vast surface area to the sun, which makes conifers especially efficient when it comes to absorbing carbon. Conifer needles and broadleaf evergreen leaves are also fibrous and often have a waxy coating that helps them survive low temperatures or dry conditions.

Deciduous leaves are more tender than evergreen leaves. Their lobes, leaflets, and jagged edges help evaporate water, reduce wind resistance, and even provide drip tips to shed rain that, left standing, could initiate disease on the leaf. When a deciduous tree drops its leaves in autumn, the tree stops expending energy and enters dormancy, which allows it to survive winter conditions.

WOOD

The trunk of a tree is made up of different layers. The outer bark is the tree's protection from the outside world. Continually renewed from within, this layer serves as a moisture barrier, insulates against extreme cold and heat, and protects the living tissues from insect damage.

The cambium is the living, growing part of the trunk. New cells produced on the outer side of the cambium become the phloem, which carries food from the leaves to the rest of the tree. Phloem cells are short-lived, becoming a part of the corky outer bark after they die. New cells produced

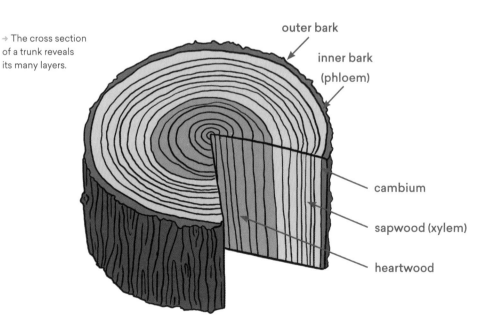

→ The cross section of a trunk reveals its many layers.

outer bark

inner bark (phloem)

cambium

sapwood (xylem)

heartwood

on the inner side of the cambium become xylem (or sapwood), which carries water and nutrients from the roots throughout the tree.

Sapwood is new wood. As newer rings of sapwood form, the innermost sapwood cells lose their vitality and turn to heartwood. While technically dead, heartwood is the hardest wood of the tree and will not decay or lose strength while the outer layers are intact—underscoring the importance of avoiding damage to a tree's trunk and branches.

Each year a tree forms a new layer of living cells arranged in concentric circles, increasing the girth of the tree. These annual growth rings show the amount of wood produced during one growing season. Spring growth is lighter, as the wood is growing quickly and consists of larger cells. In summer, growth slows and cells are smaller and darker. Collectively, these light and dark rings record the life of a tree. Count the dark rings, and you know the tree's age. Environmental conditions such as drought, fire, and insect damage are also recorded as wide or narrow rings.

ROOTS

Contrary to popular belief, the majority of tree roots are found in the top 2 to 3 feet of the soil, where most of the oxygen, water, and nutrients needed by the tree can be found. Fine short-lived feeder roots extend well beyond the dripline of a tree's canopy, often occupying an area two to four times the size of the crown. Tree roots grow when there is sufficient water, soil, and oxygen to allow for growth. They grow in all directions, but only survive and thrive when appropriate conditions are encountered. Also contrary to popular belief, few tree species have a single, deep tap root. A tree's stability and endurance depend on its outward-stretching root structure.

Larger woody roots hold the tree in place and grow in girth over time just like the trunk and branches above. The roots are critical to stability and serve as underground food-storage organs in winter. Deciduous trees lose their leaves—and their ability to produce sugars—in the fall. Even evergreen trees that retain their leaves in winter cannot perform photosynthesis well at that time of the year. When trees return from their winter dormancy in the spring, the roots release the stored foods, allowing for the leaves and buds to quickly grow and open and new leaves to emerge.

Planting a Legacy for Tomorrow

CHRISSY TAYLOR, President and CEO, Enterprise Holdings

CAROLYN KINDLE BETZ, President, Enterprise Holdings Foundation

For nearly 65 years, our family business has been synonymous with cars and travel—so we may seem unlikely contributors for a book about planting trees. But find yourself winding along a wooded mountain road or cruising along a palm-shaded coast, and you see that trees are as much a part of your trip as the road itself.

Trees breathe life into our neighborhood streets, and they bring a rich texture to our byways. Although we might not always think about it, they leave their mark on our travels. Whether driving through the California sequoias, watching the wind flicker through an aspen forest, or coasting past New England hillsides splashed with fall colors, we often know our place by the trees outside our car window. And the treetops are often the first sign of home when pulling up to the driveway at the end of a trip or a long day at the office.

At Enterprise Holdings, we're in the business of getting people where they need to go, but we've also made it our business to leave a legacy for future generations. We still remember the towering trees we climbed fearlessly as young girls. So when it came time to celebrate our company's fiftieth anniversary, we partnered with the Arbor Day Foundation to form the 50 Million Tree Pledge—an initiative to plant 50 million trees over 50 years on public lands in North America and Europe.

As Enterprise enters another year of these commitments, we find ourselves reflecting on how planting a tree is about more than just placing a seedling in the ground. It's a chance to serve our communities as a committed corporate citizen. It's a step toward improving the quality of our air, restoring our water supply, and providing a home for our wildlife. It's a lasting gift for generations to come.

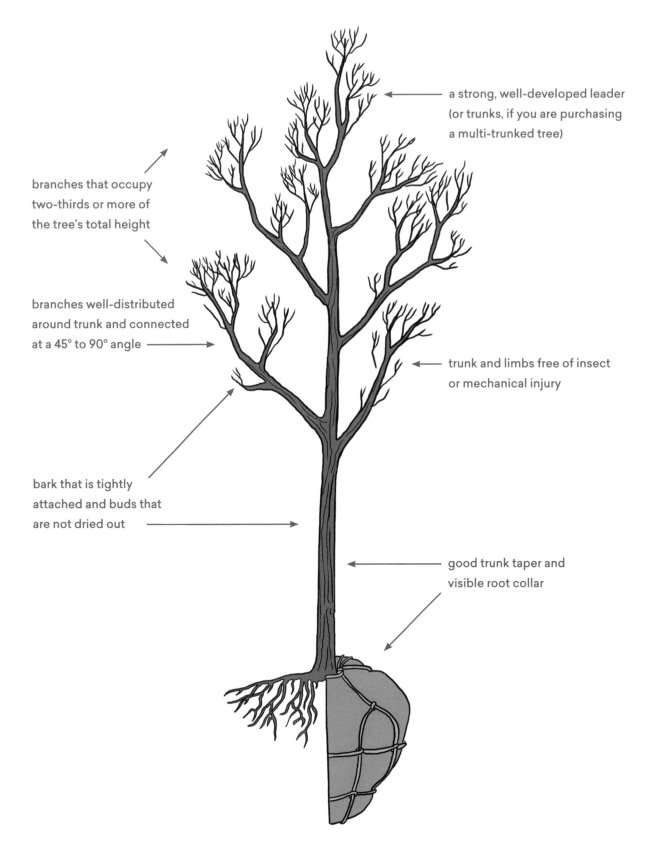

a strong, well-developed leader (or trunks, if you are purchasing a multi-trunked tree)

branches that occupy two-thirds or more of the tree's total height

branches well-distributed around trunk and connected at a 45° to 90° angle

trunk and limbs free of insect or mechanical injury

bark that is tightly attached and buds that are not dried out

good trunk taper and visible root collar

SELECTING AND PLANTING A TREE

So, you've done your homework and determined what you want in a tree and how you want it to contribute to your landscape. You've familiarized yourself with the nature of your growing region and assessed the specific conditions of your planting site. You've considered all the ways in which a tree can create a more comfortable environment, providing tangible environmental and economic benefits. You've learned about the different parts of a tree and how each of them function. Best of all, you've gotten a glimpse of the many beautiful types of trees that can enhance your landscape and transform it into a sanctuary that enriches life for everyone in your household and even your larger community. Now comes the really exciting part—selecting a heathy tree and planting it!

Good tree care starts with choosing a healthy tree. Remember, your tree will be with you for years, maybe even generations, to come. Here's what to look for when purchasing a tree to ensure that it gets off to a healthy start and can provide a lifetime of benefits.

SHOPPING FOR TREES

When shopping for trees at the nursery, choosing a tree with a strong central leader is especially important for shade trees. Avoid trees with multiple leaders. Low branches, while temporary, help promote growth and protect plant from sun scald—so be sure they look healthy as well.

At the nursery, you'll find plants have been categorized based on how they were produced, harvested, and prepared for retail. The various options, which include container-grown trees, ball-and-burlap specimens, and bare root plants, require different handling and planting techniques.

Container-grown trees have spent their entire nursery life growing in a container. A well-tended container-grown tree has been carefully monitored and moved up into gradually larger containers as the plant grows. If a tree outgrows its container without being moved up, its roots will begin to circle or twist within the container, which may lead to girdling, or strangling the plant's vascular system, and root die-off.

It's perfectly acceptable to gently remove a tree from its container at the nursery to inspect the roots. Roots will continue to grow in the direction they are already pointing. Fine circling roots may be untangled or cut away at planting. Larger, woody roots may be straightened if they are still flexible.

↑ Container-grown trees are cultivated in pots.

↑ Ball-and-burlap trees are dug from the field and wrapped for transport.

Container-grown trees may be planted at any point in the year provided the soil is workable and not frozen, knowing that the hottest days will require frequent watering.

Ball-and-burlap trees are grown in the ground until they have achieved a targeted size. When a tree is ready to be moved, the root ball is dug along with a mass of surrounding soil, then wrapped in burlap in preparation for transporting and resale. Larger root balls may be further supported by a wire basket cage over the burlap.

When purchasing a ball-and-burlap tree, look for a firm root ball that is securely tied. It's critically important that the root ball is large enough to support the maturity of the tree; it should be about 10 to 12 inches wide for every 1 inch of trunk diameter measured at a point 6 inches above the root collar. Avoid buying plants with damaged or compressed root balls; rounded or misshapen root balls may indicate woody root loss.

Always carry a ball-and-burlap tree while supporting the root ball. Moving or lifting the tree by its trunk may cause the root ball to separate from the trunk.

Because ball-and-burlap trees are dug from a nursery field, most of the root system has been removed. Don't worry, though, they will quickly regrow a functioning root system. But that means ball-and-burlap trees should be planted during cooler weather, avoiding the hottest, most stressful time of year.

HOW TO READ A PLANT LABEL

Plant taxonomists are scientists who classify and group plants. Botanical nomenclature, a richly descriptive scientific naming convention understood across all languages, is constructed to clearly communicate identifying details about a plant. While the system is complicated, reading a plant label doesn't have to be.

- A **genus** is a group of plants that have fundamental traits in common but that differ in other lesser characteristics. The genus name (such as *Acer*) is capitalized and italic.

- A **species** is a natural subset within a genus describing an individual trait that breeds true, that is, remains consistent from generation to generation. The species name (such as *rubrum*) is lowercase and italic.

- A **variety** (var.) is a subdivision of a species having a distinct, stable trait that differs from what is typical for the species.

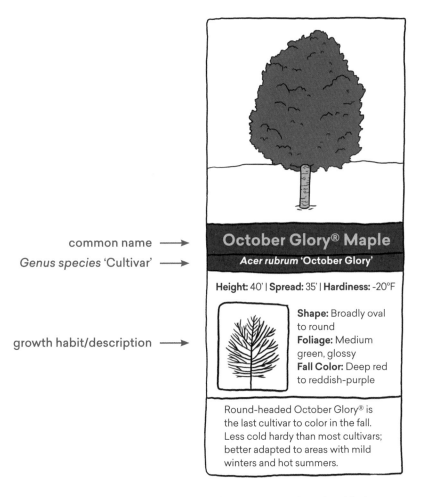

common name →
Genus species 'Cultivar' →

growth habit/description →

October Glory® Maple
Acer rubrum 'October Glory'

Height: 40' | **Spread:** 35' | **Hardiness:** -20°F

Shape: Broadly oval to round
Foliage: Medium green, glossy
Fall Color: Deep red to reddish-purple

Round-headed October Glory® is the last cultivar to color in the fall. Less cold hardy than most cultivars; better adapted to areas with mild winters and hot summers.

↑ Plant labels contain lots of useful information.

- A **cultivar** is a named cultivated variety selected for one or more outstanding characteristics that is vegetatively reproduced, or cloned, to preserve specific genetics. The cultivar name (such as 'October Glory') is capitalized and written in single quotes.

A plant label offers a tremendous amount of valuable information that you can use to choose the attributes you're looking for in a tree. For instance, a plant labeled *Acer rubrum* 'October Glory' is a red maple with particularly brilliant fall color that will be identical to other cultivars of the same name. Plant labels also provide details about a tree's growth pattern, sun requirements, watering needs, and any special soil requirements.

Labels in the landscape can be an eyesore. Remove the label from your tree after planting, but be sure to keep it somewhere safe for future reference.

↑ If placing the tree in a lawn, remove a circle at least 3 feet in diameter for your new tree.

PREPARATION IS EVERYTHING

After making sure that you select a healthy, well-formed tree, properly preparing your planting site is the best thing you can do to get your tree off to a strong start.

Before you plant, make sure your tree is thoroughly hydrated by watering the container or root ball several hours before proceeding; it's very difficult to rewet a large root ball that has dried out after the tree has been planted.

When planting a tree into a lawn, remove a circle of grass at least 3 feet in diameter where the tree will go to reduce competition between turf and fine tree roots. In areas where the lawn is the primary design feature, select small trees with open canopies that will allow sunlight to penetrate to the ground. Remove turf altogether where surface tree roots—most prevalent where topsoil is compacted—may be damaged in the future by mowing.

PLANTING CONTAINER-GROWN AND BALL-AND-BURLAP TREES

Gather your tools. You'll need a measuring tape or ruler to help guide you in digging your planting hole and placing the root ball at the proper depth. The majority of a young tree's roots develop in the top 12 inches of soil, where water and oxygen are most accessible. If the tree is planted too deeply, new roots will have difficulty developing due to a lack of oxygen. In poorly drained or heavy clay soils, trees can be planted with the base of the root collar above grade—1 inch for every inch of trunk diameter.

──────────────── YOU'LL NEED ────────────────

measuring tape or ruler

spade or shovel

tarp

wire cutters
(for ball-and-burlap trees)

pocket knife or hand pruners

a bag of mulch

- Measure the root ball, either in the container or ball-and-burlap, to determine how wide and how deep of a planting hole to dig for your tree.

- Dig a broad, shallow planting hole with gently sloping sides that is three to four times wider than the diameter of the root mass and the same depth. Mounding removed soil on a tarp makes backfilling and clean up a snap. Further loosening the soil on the sloping sides of the planting hole allows roots to easily expand and establish faster, but don't disturb soil at the bottom of the hole.

- If you are planting a containerized tree, prepare the root ball for planting. Sharply tap the outside of the container to loosen and remove the root ball from the container, being careful to keep the soil around the roots intact. You may need to slice the plastic pot, from lip to bottom, to facilitate loosening the root ball. To remedy circling or congested roots, use a sharp knife to carefully slice an X across the bottom of the root ball and make four vertical slices along the sides of the soil mass. This will encourage roots to branch at the point where they were cut and move out into the surrounding soil.

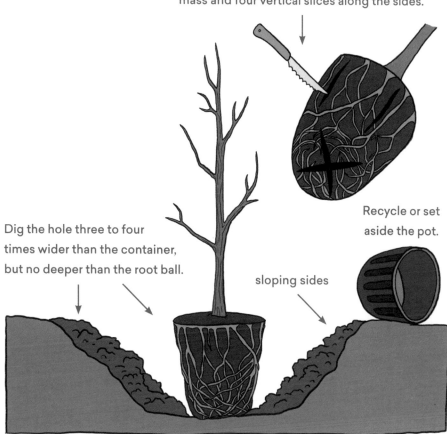

If root bound, cut an X across the bottom of the root mass and four vertical slices along the sides.

Recycle or set aside the pot.

Dig the hole three to four times wider than the container, but no deeper than the root ball.

sloping sides

↑ The first steps in planting a container-grown tree

- Set your tree in the middle of the planting hole. Remember to lift by supporting the root ball. Don't pull on the trunk or the roots may separate from the tree. Double check to make sure that the planting hole has been dug to the proper depth and no deeper. The root collar should be just above soil level; if it's too low, compact soil beneath the root ball to raise it to the correct level.

- For ball-and-burlap trees, once the root ball is in position, use wire cutters to cut vertically up the side of the wire basket and peel it away. Remove all rope or twine from the root ball as well as any nails that may be holding the burlap together. Pull the burlap away from the top and sides of the root ball and cut away any loose material. Don't worry about regular burlap under the root ball, because it will naturally break down over time. But vinyl or coated burlap should be removed completely.

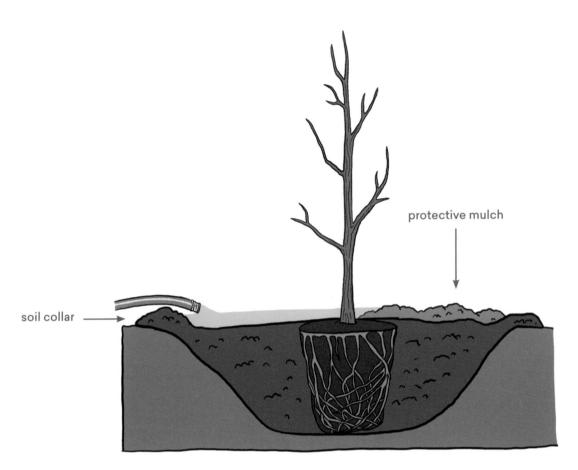

protective mulch

soil collar

↑ The final steps in planting a container-grown tree

- Straighten the tree in the hole. Before backfilling, have someone view the tree from several directions to confirm that the tree is straight. As you can imagine, it is very difficult to reposition a tree once it's planted.

- Replace the soil, while firmly but gently tamping the original soil around the base of the root ball to stabilize it. Do not amend the backfill or apply fertilizer at planting time. Keep backfilling until the soil is just below the root collar.

- Create a water-holding basin around the tree by building up a ring of soil—or flip over the grass you removed to make room for the tree and build a ring with that—and then water thoroughly to settle roots and eliminate air pockets that may cause roots to dry out.

- Spread protective mulch 2 to 4 inches deep in a 3-foot diameter area around the base of the tree, but not touching the trunk.

- Other than removing dead and broken limbs, avoid pruning your tree at planting.

Bare root trees are sold with no soil surrounding their roots. Like ball-and-burlap stock, these trees are field grown and then dug and prepared for sale while the plant is dormant. Each winter, many retail nurseries receive inventory as bare root stock and pass along generous discounts before potting trees into containers in preparation for their busy spring shopping season. Some mail order nurseries offer bare root trees during winter as a way to save on shipping costs. Roots are dipped in hydrating gel prior to shipping to keep them moist and healthy.

Bare root trees with abundant fibrous roots get off to a vigorous start compared to ball-and-burlap or container-grown trees, which typically need more time to adjust to transplanting. This vigor means bare root trees may surpass the size of larger containerized stock in only a few years.

← Bare root trees are sold with no soil surrounding their roots.

While the savings can be substantial when purchasing a bare root tree, it's a false economy if your tree doesn't survive. The planting window for bare root trees is limited. The tree should be planted in the ground while it is still dormant, before fine annual feeding roots initiate growth in early spring and warming weather stimulates top growth.

YOU'LL NEED

bucket

tarp

measuring tape or ruler

pocket knife or hand pruners

spade or shovel

a bag of mulch

- When purchasing a bare root tree, check to make sure that the roots are not dried out; all cuts should be clean, with no sign of tearing or decay. If your tree has been ordered by mail, remove all packing material and carefully untangle the roots. Soak the roots in a bucket of water for 3 to 6 hours.

SELECTING AND PLANTING A TREE

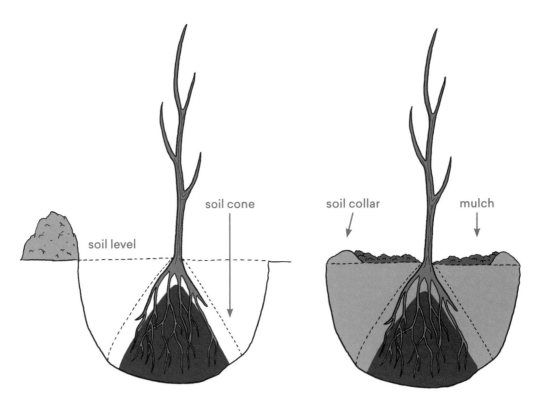

soil cone

soil collar

mulch

soil level

↑ Planting a bare root tree

- If planting in a lawn, remove turf and loosen the soil within a 3-foot circular area. Dig a hole that is wider than seems necessary, so the roots can easily grow outward without crowding. Mounding removed soil on a tarp makes clean up a snap.

- Build a soil cone in the hole so that, when the tree is placed on top of it, the root collar is just above soil level. Spread the roots over and around the soil cone. Partially fill the hole, firming the soil around the lower roots to stabilize the tree. Do not amend the backfill or apply fertilizer at planting time.

- Replace the remaining soil, and water the loose soil around the roots to eliminate air pockets until the soil is just below the root collar.

- Create a water-holding basin around the tree by building up a collar of soil, and water thoroughly to settle roots and eliminate air pockets that may cause roots to dry out.

- Spread mulch 2 to 4 inches deep in a 3-foot diameter area around the base of the tree, but not touching the trunk.

↑ Keep newly planted trees watered well for the first year after planting.

TENDING TO YOUR NEWLY PLANTED TREE

How you care for your tree in its first and early years of life will affect its shape, strength, and even its life span. It's hard to get a tree to its second year if it doesn't live through its first. The best thing you can do for a newly planted tree is to keep it watered well during the first year after planting. You'll want to water it weekly so that the soil stays moist, but not soggy. A simple trick is to stick your thumb in the soil. If it comes out dry or dusty, the tree needs water. If it comes out muddy, then it doesn't need water.

In dry spells, water the entire area within a little beyond the drip line to keep soil and mulch moist but not soggy; avoid waterlogged conditions. Water the tree about once a week, enough to have the soil damp to a depth of 1 to 3 feet, depending on the tree's size. Mulching with wood chips, bark, or other organic material helps retain soil moisture and reduces competition from weeds and grass.

Studies have shown that trees establish more quickly and develop stronger trunks and root systems if they are *not* staked at the time of planting. However, staking may be required for bare root stock and container-grown

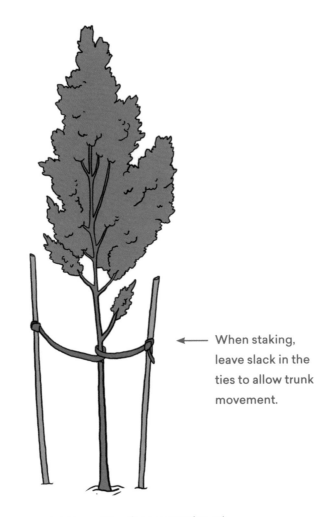

When staking, leave slack in the ties to allow trunk movement.

↑ Remove support staking and ties after one year of growth.

conifers or when planting on windy sites. Stakes can also prevent lawn mower damage. If you decide to stake, use two opposing flexible straps placed as low on the tree as possible to perform the task. The tree should be able to sway in the wind—without the root ball moving— which aids trunk and root development. Check support staking regularly for damage to the trunk and remove all straps and ties after the first year of growth.

It's important that tree roots expand and establish in the native soil. Soil properties are extremely difficult to change with an amendment of any kind. Do not add potting soil or organic or chemical fertilizer on your newly planted trees, which can cause waterlogging or burn roots.

Keep vines away from newly planted trees, and remove all tags and labels. Not only are labels an eyesore in the landscape, leaving them in place can strangle limbs as the tree grows. After you remove them, keep labels somewhere safe for future reference.

PRUNING

The wisdom of pruning young trees is often ignored, possibly because it is difficult to think ahead and envision what a tree will look like in the coming years. How you prune a tree during its first few years will affect its shape, strength, and even its life span. Proper pruning will save you money and give you trees that are safer, healthier, more attractive, and easier to maintain.

Although light pruning and the removal of dead or broken branches can be done anytime, there are limits to how much you can afford to prune before the tree's overall health suffers. Trees need as many leaves as possible to maintain a healthy growth rate. A general rule is to remove no more than 20–25 percent of live branches and that, after pruning, two-thirds of the height of the tree should still have branches and leaves. It's better to manage your trees with an annual pruning cycle, beginning 2 to 3 years after planting, than to try and play catch up after early neglect.

Safety should always be your number one priority. Use a pole pruner to make cuts on high branches. Contact an insured, certified arborist if pruning requires removing large branches (greater than 4 inches in diameter), running a chainsaw overhead, or removing entire trees or trees near a structure.

↓ Proper pruning begins 2–3 years after planting but the tools and techniques will be used for the life of the tree.

KEYS TO GOOD PRUNING

Pruning allows you to shape a tree and enhance its beauty in the landscape. Every pruning cut you make should have a reason: safety, tree health, or aesthetics.

- Keep your tools sharp. One-hand pruning shears with curved blades (secateurs) or a pruning saw work best on young trees. To limit disease transmission, dip your tools in a 10 percent bleach solution (1 cup bleach to 9 cups water) or 70 percent isopropyl alcohol between cuts or between trees. Once you're done, rinse and dry tools before storing.

- Prune early in the life of the tree to direct growth and to keep pruning wounds small to limit the chance of decay. However, do not start pruning until 2 or 3 years after planting. A new transplant needs its leaves to produce strong new growth.

- Before you begin, inspect your tree from the top and work downward, identifying the central leader and lateral branches. Identify and retain lateral branches that form 10 o'clock or 2 o'clock angles with the trunk. Branches at these angles will be stronger than those with sharper angles.

- Remove diseased or damaged parts of a tree before pruning for structure.

- Don't worry about coating pruning cuts. Wound dressing is unnecessary and ill-advised, unless you are pruning live or red oaks in an area where oak wilt is present. In that case, and more generally for aesthetics, you should coat wounds with a neutral-colored latex paint within 15 minutes of making a cut. This will prevent disease transmission, but research shows that it does not prevent or reduce decay. Only the size of the cut can limit decay.

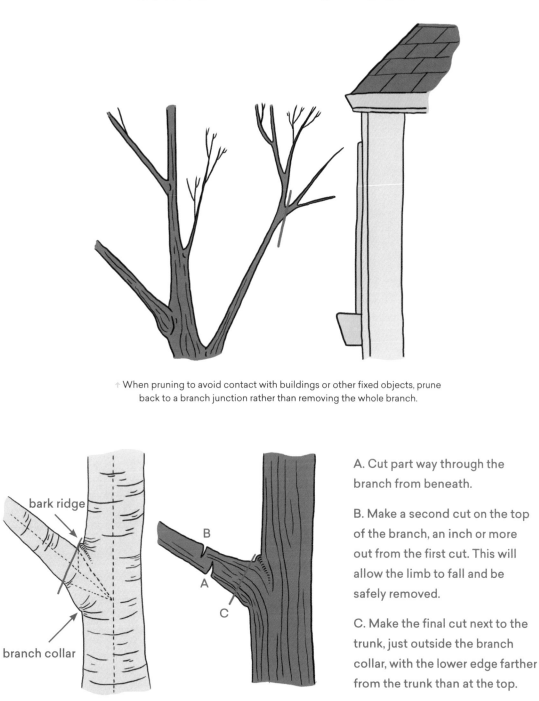

↑ When pruning to avoid contact with buildings or other fixed objects, prune back to a branch junction rather than removing the whole branch.

A. Cut part way through the branch from beneath.

B. Make a second cut on the top of the branch, an inch or more out from the first cut. This will allow the limb to fall and be safely removed.

C. Make the final cut next to the trunk, just outside the branch collar, with the lower edge farther from the trunk than at the top.

↑ Large, heavy limbs could tear loose during pruning, stripping bark and creating wounds that invite insects and disease. That won't happen if you follow these steps.

PRUNING

PRUNE WITH AN EYE TO THE FUTURE

Branches do not move up the trunk as the tree grows. A branch that is 5 feet from the ground now will be 5 feet off the ground in 10 years—only thicker and longer than it is now. Try to visualize what a particular branch will look like later and remove any branches that will cause a problem. Prune shade trees as lightly as possible. Never remove more than one-fourth of a tree's crown in a season.

↑ Select a single leader and protect it from competition. Remove codominant leaders.

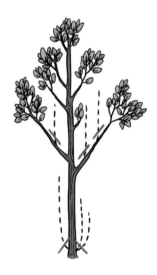

↑ Suckers and water sprouts are rapidly growing, weakly attached, vertical branches that can appear at the base of the tree or in the crown. Remove them as soon as possible.

Unless they are broken, leave lower branches on for the first year.

↑ Newly planted tree

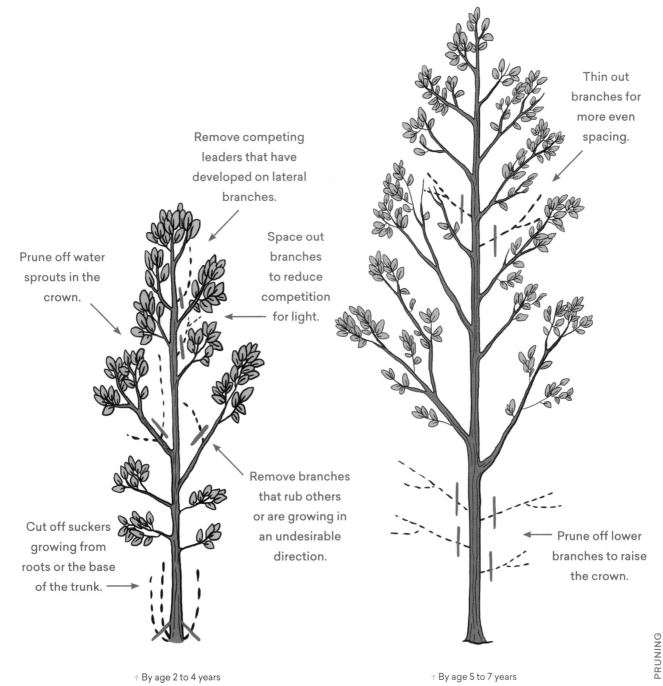

Remove competing leaders that have developed on lateral branches.

Space out branches to reduce competition for light.

Prune off water sprouts in the crown.

Remove branches that rub others or are growing in an undesirable direction.

Cut off suckers growing from roots or the base of the trunk.

↑ By age 2 to 4 years

Thin out branches for more even spacing.

Prune off lower branches to raise the crown.

↑ By age 5 to 7 years

PRUNING

↑ When you prune will determine how your tree responds.

WHEN TO PRUNE

Trees need care in every season. When to prune depends on why you are pruning, but corrective pruning—removing diseased or broken limbs and those that impose a hazard—may be performed at any time of the year.

WINTER Pruning during dormancy is the most common practice, since the branch arrangement is most visible at this time. It's usually best to wait until the coldest part of the winter has passed. Trees such as maples, walnuts, and birches may "bleed" when the sap begins to flow. This is not harmful and will stop when the tree leafs out.

SPRING AND SUMMER Prune spring-flowering species after they have finished flowering. Removing or reducing branches during spring and summer can be used to direct growth on the fastest-growing species. For most trees, pruning during the growing season reduces photosynthesis and diminishes the amount of food being manufactured and stored for future growing seasons, effectively curbing growth. Another reason to prune in summer is for corrective purposes, removing or shortening fast-growing limbs and those that hang down too far under the weight of their leaves.

FALL This is a good time to keep your pruning tools in storage. As growth slows at the end of the growing season, pruning wounds close more slowly and are subject to invasion by decay-causing fungi that spread their spores profusely in fall.

TREE HEALTH GUIDE

Spring is a great time to check the health of the trees in your landscape. The canopy of deciduous trees has yet to fill in, and you can clearly see the structure of the tree and identify damage from winter storms. Not sure where to begin? Use this spring tree health checklist to identify possible factors limiting tree growth and development. If you notice one or more of these problems, contact your local nursery professional or consult with a certified arborist.

CHECK BRANCHES Look for broken or dangling branches or cracks where branches attach to the trunk. Branches that are missing bark or growing fungus can be signs of decaying wood and indicate potential problems. However, don't worry about moss, ferns, and lichen growing on branches; that's simply a sign of a healthy relationship between trees and their environment. Narrow angles at the point where a branch grows from the trunk are structurally weak and prone to breaking; this is especially common with elm and maple trees.

CHECK LEAVES As spring progresses, the tree should leaf out evenly with healthy looking foliage. Uneven coloring or slow growth in portions of the tree are warning signs. Most mature trees need little fertilizer, but specific nutrient deficiencies indicated by poor or uneven foliage color may need to be corrected. You should also check leaves for signs of insect damage.

CHECK ROOTS Fungus or mushroom growth on large anchoring roots, along the base of the trunk, or on soil near the tree can indicate decay. Cavities or hollows near the base of the tree or in large roots can also be a sign of trouble. Cracked or raised soil on one side of a tree trunk could indicate the start of leaning and weakness. New construction and soil compaction can also damage roots.

CHECK TRUNKS Look for cracks or cavities, oozing wounds, or sunken or missing bark. Again, mushrooms or fungal growth can also be a sign of decay and structural weakness. Any of these symptoms can diminish a tree's stability. The exterior of a tree may appear fine except for a small crack, cavity, or fungus while the interior may be rotted, soft, or even empty. If you notice one or more of these problems, consult with a certified arborist.

WHEN TO CALL AN ARBORIST

Arborists are professional tree care providers who are trained in the art and science of planting, caring for, and maintaining trees. The International Society of Arboriculture is a network of professional researchers, arborists, and tree care leaders who bring science and expertise to trees. Their work helps to drive public awareness, professional development, and the latest research on tree care and tree management around the globe.

There are two types of professional arborists: certified and consulting. Certified arborists are trained to offer advice and services for planting, pruning, transplanting, fertilizing, monitoring and treatment for insects and diseases, and tree removal. Consulting arborists specialize in diagnosing problems, recommending treatments, tree appraisals, and connecting homeowners with competent tree service providers.

When you suspect problems or are looking for expert advice on caring for your tree, it's time to call an arborist. Pruning and removing trees, especially large trees, is dangerous. Tree work should be done only by those trained and equipped to work safely in trees.

An arborist can provide the following services:

PLANTING Some arborists plant trees, and most can recommend species that are appropriate for a particular location.

PRUNING An arborist can determine the type of pruning necessary to maintain or improve the health, appearance, and safety of trees.

PLANT HEALTHCARE An arborist can recommend a preventive maintenance routine to keep trees in good health while reducing any insect, disease, or site problems.

↑ Know when to call in a tree professional.

TENDING MATURE TREES An arborist can offer consulting services, tree risk assessment, cabling and bracing, and other methods of caring for a mature tree.

EMERGENCY TREE CARE An arborist can assist in performing emergency tree care in a safe manner, while reducing further risk of damage to property.

TREE REMOVAL An arborist can help decide whether a tree should be removed. Although tree removal is a last resort, there are circumstances when it is necessary.

With global exploration, transportation, and trade, the spread of plants, animals, and pathogens beyond their natural range is inevitable. The commercial nursery industry has introduced countless non-native plants that enhance our landscapes with beauty and support local ecosystems. But what works in one region may not be sustainable under other conditions. When an introduced plant becomes invasive, the impact on the environment can be detrimental or even disastrous.

Invasive plants are known to reproduce rapidly and spread quickly, displacing native species when unchecked by natural controls such as animals, insects, or diseases to stop their spread. Newly introduced insects or disease pathogens put pressure on organisms that haven't yet developed resistance. All invasive species pose a threat to biological diversity.

Like invasiveness, tree diseases and pests vary tremendously from region to region. In addition, what's ailing a tree is often difficult to diagnose. When questions come up, reach out to a regional nursery professional or other knowledgeable expert familiar with local growing conditions to help you find answers.

The local office of the U.S. Department of Agriculture's Cooperative Extension Service is one of the best resources for assistance with home gardening disease and pest questions, offering trusted research-based knowledge. With the help of volunteer Master Gardeners, extension agents can quickly answer most inquiries about plant healthcare and local conditions, including information about potentially invasive species in your area. Below you will find some basic information about what may be affecting your tree's health.

DROUGHT

Drought is a common issue affecting trees across the country. Lack of water can cause a wide range of issues including leaf wilting, leaf scorch, stem dieback, and increased susceptibility to pests and diseases. In dry spells, water the entire area within a little beyond the drip line to keep soil and mulch moist but not soggy; avoid waterlogged conditions. Water the tree about once a week, enough to have the soil damp to a depth of 1 to 3 feet, depending on the tree's size. Mulching with wood chips, bark, or other organic material helps retain soil moisture and reduces competition from weeds and grass.

DISEASES

Diseases can vary greatly based on the type of tree and the region it grows in. Some of the more common diseases facing trees in the United States are listed below.

DOGWOOD ANTHRACNOSE affects flowering and Pacific dogwoods. Symptoms of this fungal disease include spots with tan centers and reddish purple margins on the leaves and distorted, wilted, and curled foliage. Stem and branch cankers may also appear.

DUTCH ELM DISEASE affects American elms, winged elms, September elms, slippery elms, rock elms, and cedar elms to varying degrees. This often-fatal fungal disease is spread by bark beetles. The first sign is that the leaves on one or more branches of a stricken tree suddenly wilt, turn yellow and then brown, curl, and drop early.

EASTERN FILBERT BLIGHT affects hazelnuts. This fungal disease produces raised bumps on bark that are white early in the growing season and later become black. These bumps appear in straight rows along the length of branches.

OAK WILT affects many species of oaks. It is a fungal disease spread by boring beetles or root-to-root contact with an infected tree. Symptoms include leaves of entire branches turning yellow or brown and the shedding of green leaves with brown veins.

PINE WILT affects non-native pines such as Austrian, Scots, and Japanese red and black pines. This rapidly fatal disease is caused by a parasitic nematode that feeds on cells of the tree's vascular system. Needles change first to grayish green, then tan and brown, with the discoloration moving from the top of the tree downward.

SUDDEN OAK DEATH kills tanoaks, coast live oaks, Shreve's oaks, California black oaks and canyon live oaks; the disease also affects Douglasfirs, coast redwoods, madrones, and many other trees. Early symptoms include weeping cankers on the trunk, which eventually leads to crown death. The fungus that causes this disease is a quarantined pathogen, so do not bring material from the tree off-site for diagnosis.

THOUSAND CANKERS DISEASE affects black walnuts. This fungal disease is spread by beetles, and the first sign of infection is the outer bark around their entrance holes becoming dark and cracks forming in the bark of smaller branches. As the disease progresses, more visible symptoms include yellowing of the leaves and upper crown thinning.

PESTS

Tree-damaging pests to look out for also depend on the type of tree and your growing region. These are some common pests that attack trees in North America.

ASIAN CITRUS PSYLLID is a mottled brown insect about the size of an aphid that spreads a bacterial disease of citrus trees around the world. The adult feeds with its head down, almost touching the leaf, with the rest of its body is raised from the surface. White waxy excretions are a sign of this insect.

ASIAN LONGHORNED BEETLE adults have a bullet-shaped, shiny black body with white spots, measuring from ¾ to 1½ inches in length. The long, striped antennae are 1.5 to 2.5 times the size of the body. This destructive beetle leaves pencil-sized, perfectly round exit holes, and it is a serious pest of eastern hardwoods. Although uncommon, this beetle is regionally important where control measures are underway.

BARK BEETLES are tiny insects with hard, cylindrical bodies that reproduce under the bark of trees. Most of the 600 species in the United States live in dead, dying, or weakened hosts.

EMERALD ASH BORER is devastating some of the country's most valuable woodland and landscape trees, and all native species in the ash genus (*Fraxinus*) are susceptible. Adult borers usually emerge in mid to late May. The bright metallic green beetles are typically ½ inch long and ⅛ inch wide.

GYPSY MOTH larvae are voracious eaters, and a bad infestation can defoliate a tree in a matter of days. The caterpillars measure up to 2¾ inches long. They are hairy, black or brown, and have five pairs of blue bumps toward the front and six pairs of red bumps toward the back. This pest affects hundreds of species of plants, but oaks and aspens are most favored.

HEMLOCK WOOLLY ADELGID is a tiny aphid-like insect that attacks hemlock forest and landscape trees. This pest can be easily identified on a hemlock tree by the white woolly masses that form on the underside of branches at the base of the needles.

→ JAPANESE BEETLE feeds on hundreds of species of woody and nonwoody plants east of the Rockies. It is a scarab beetle with an iridescent copper-colored body and a green thorax and head.

**NATIVE SPECIES, YES.
INVASIVE SPECIES, NO.**

→ Pin oak acorns are eaten by many songbirds, wild turkeys, white-tailed deer, squirrels, and smaller rodents, but they are a particularly important food for many ducks.

The Arbor Day Foundation works closely with many partners and peers including the International Society of Arboriculture, the U.S. Forest Service, the National Association of State Foresters, leading experts in academia, and many other organizations to best inform tree planters on planting the right trees in the right place for the right reasons. Our guidelines are:

- Whenever practical, plant native species. Native tree species are vital for the food web of insects, birds, and other wildlife.

- Avoid planting invasive species. *Non-native* isn't the same as *invasive*. There are many well-behaved non-native species that are beneficial. Consult with trusted local tree experts to find out which tree species are recommended in your area.

- Plant a diversity of tree species. Tree diversity helps mitigate the damage that's possible when only a few species dominate a landscape. For example, devastating widespread tree loss resulting from Dutch elm disease and emerald ash borer could have been reduced with greater species diversity. What's more, a diversity of tree species can often lead to a diversity of songbirds and other wildlife. To accomplish diversity, especially in urban landscapes, non-natives should sometimes be included to complement the native species that are available.

- Depending on your goals, well-adapted, well-behaved, beneficial non-native trees may be the best option. For example, when there isn't enough space for an American linden, consider a non-native little-leaf linden. It's a good choice when habitat for pollinators is a goal. And some of the ecological benefits of a North American native elm can be realized with a non-native lacebark elm, for example, especially in urban environments.

A CALL TO ACTION

Thanks for being a part of Time for Trees. Along with all of my colleagues at the Arbor Day Foundation, I'm enthusiastic and optimistic about the tree planting movement that's emerging around the world. Trees and tree planters are planting change. Spread the word.

Share your trees! Post pictures on Instagram, Facebook, or Twitter, and tag them with #ArborDay.

CHAPTER 7

TREES FOR HOMEOWNERS

The following tree chart is designed to help you select the best tree for your landscape. ▶

Each tree is listed by botanical and common name and coded to indicate where it will grow and thrive. Information about growth habit, whether the tree is deciduous or evergreen, what shape its canopy will be, and how fast or how slow you can expect the tree to grow is also included to help you fine tune your decision-making process.

While every tree on this list is recommended by the tree experts at the Arbor Day Foundation, it's not an exhaustive list. Consult with local tree experts and nursery professionals to determine additional trees that are well suited to your growing conditions.

Welcome to the wide world of trees. Let's get planting.

NOTE

NW: Northwest

N: North

SW: Southwest

SP: Southern Plains

MW: Midwest

S: South

MA: Mid-Atlantic

NE: Northeast

TR: Tropical

SMALL: less than 25 feet

MEDIUM: 25 to 40 feet

LARGE: greater than 40 feet

Botanical name	Common name	Growing region									Tree type	Tree shape	Growth rate	Tree size
		NW	N	SW	SP	MW	S	MA	NE	TR				
Abies concolor	white fir (concolor fir)	◆	◆			◆		◆	◆		evergreen	pyramidal	slow to medium	large
Acacia baileyana	Bailey acacia			◆	◆						deciduous	rounded	medium to fast	medium
Acer griseum	paperbark maple	◆	◆			◆		◆	◆		deciduous	oval	medium	small
Acer palmatum	Japanese red maple	◆	◆			◆	◆	◆	◆		deciduous	rounded	slow to medium	small
Acer rubrum	red maple	◆	◆		◆	◆	◆	◆	◆		deciduous	oval	medium to fast	large
Acer saccharum	sugar maple	◆	◆			◆		◆	◆		deciduous	oval	slow to medium	large
Aesculus glabra	Ohio buckeye	◆	◆			◆		◆	◆		deciduous	oval	slow to medium	medium
Aesculus hippocastanum	horsechestnut	◆	◆			◆		◆	◆		deciduous	rounded	medium	large
Amelanchier canadensis	shadblow serviceberry	◆	◆		◆	◆	◆	◆	◆		deciduous	rounded	medium	small
Arbutus unedo	strawberry tree	◆	◆	◆							evergreen	rounded	slow	medium
Asimina triloba	pawpaw	◆	◆		◆	◆	◆	◆			deciduous	rounded	medium	small
Bauhinia variegata	purple orchid tree			◆	◆		◆			◆	semi-evergreen	rounded	medium	medium
Betula nigra	river birch	◆	◆		◆	◆	◆	◆			deciduous	oval	medium to fast	large
Betula papyrifera	paper birch	◆	◆			◆		◆	◆		deciduous	oval	medium to fast	large
Bourreria succulenta	Bahama strongbark									◆	evergreen	rounded	medium	small
Callistemon rigidus	red bottlebrush			◆	◆		◆			◆	evergreen	pyramidal	medium	small
Capparis cynophallophora	Jamaican caper									◆	evergreen	vase	slow	small

Botanical name	Common name	Growing region									Tree type	Tree shape	Growth rate	Tree size
		NW	N	SW	SP	MW	S	MA	NE	TR				
Carpinus caroliniana	American hornbeam	◆	◆		◆	◆	◆	◆	◆		deciduous	rounded	slow	medium
Carya illinoinensis	pecan			◆	◆	◆	◆				deciduous	oval	medium	large
Carya laciniosa	shellbark hickory		◆			◆		◆	◆		deciduous	oval	slow	large
Catalpa speciosa	northern catalpa	◆	◆			◆		◆	◆		deciduous	oval	medium to fast	large
Cedrus atlantica	Atlas cedar	◆			◆	◆	◆	◆			evergreen	pyramidal	slow	large
Cedrus deodara	deodar cedar			◆	◆		◆	◆			evergreen	pyramidal	medium	large
Celtis occidentalis	northern hackberry	◆	◆			◆		◆	◆		deciduous	rounded	medium to fast	large
Cercidiphyllum japonicum	katsura tree					◆		◆	◆		deciduous	rounded	slow to medium	large
Cercis canadensis	eastern redbud	◆	◆			◆	◆	◆	◆		deciduous	rounded	medium	medium
Cercis canadensis var. texensis	Texas redbud			◆	◆					◆	deciduous	vase	fast	medium
Chilopsis linearis	desert-willow			◆	◆		◆			◆	deciduous	vase	medium	small
Chionanthus virginicus	white fringetree					◆	◆	◆	◆		deciduous	rounded	medium	small
Cinnamomum camphora	camphor tree			◆	◆		◆			◆	evergreen	rounded	fast	large
Cladrastis kentukea	yellowwood	◆	◆			◆	◆	◆	◆		deciduous	rounded	medium	large
Cordia boissieri	Texas olive			◆	◆					◆	evergreen	rounded	fast	small
Cornus florida	flowering dogwood	◆	◆		◆	◆	◆	◆	◆		deciduous	rounded	medium	small

Botanical name	Common name	Growing region									Tree type	Tree shape	Growth rate	Tree size
		NW	N	SW	SP	MW	S	MA	NE	TR				
Cornus kousa	Kousa dogwood (Japanese dogwood)	◆	◆		◆	◆	◆	◆	◆		deciduous	rounded	slow to medium	small
Cornus mas	cornelian cherry dogwood	◆	◆			◆		◆	◆		deciduous	rounded	medium	small
Crataegus phaenopyrum	Washington hawthorn	◆	◆		◆	◆	◆	◆	◆		deciduous	pyramidal	medium	medium
Cupressus arizonica	Arizona cypress			◆	◆	◆	◆	◆			evergreen	pyramidal	medium	large
Cupressus sempervirens	Italian cypress			◆	◆		◆	◆		◆	evergreen	columnar	medium	large
Cuprocyparis leylandii	Leyland cypress	◆			◆	◆	◆	◆			evergreen	pyramidal	fast	large
Dermato-phyllum secundiflorum	Texas mountain laurel (mescalbean)			◆	◆						evergreen	rounded	slow	small
Diospyros virginiana	common persimmon	◆	◆		◆	◆	◆	◆	◆		deciduous	oval	medium	large
Ebenopsis ebano	Texas ebony			◆	◆					◆	evergreen	rounded	slow to medium	large
Eriobotrya deflexa	bronze loquat			◆						◆	evergreen	rounded	fast	small
Eucommia ulmoides	hardy rubber tree	◆	◆		◆	◆		◆	◆		deciduous	rounded	medium	large
Eugenia foetida	Spanish stopper									◆	evergreen	vase	medium	small
Fagus grandifolia	American beech	◆	◆			◆		◆	◆		deciduous	oval	slow to medium	large
Ficus carica	common fig			◆	◆		◆			◆	deciduous	rounded	medium	small
Ginkgo biloba	ginkgo	◆	◆		◆	◆	◆	◆	◆		deciduous	pyramidal	medium	large
Gleditsia triacanthos var. inermis	thornless honeylocust	◆	◆	◆	◆	◆	◆	◆	◆		deciduous	oval	fast	large

Botanical name	Common name	Growing region									Tree type	Tree shape	Growth rate	Tree size
		NW	N	SW	SP	MW	S	MA	NE	TR				
Gymnocladus dioicus	Kentucky coffeetree	◆	◆		◆	◆	◆	◆	◆		deciduous	oval	slow to medium	large
Ilex cassine	dahoon holly				◆		◆			◆	evergreen	oval	medium	medium
Ilex vomitoria	yaupon holly			◆	◆		◆				evergreen	vase	medium	small
Jacaranda mimosifolia	jacaranda			◆						◆	deciduous	rounded	fast	large
Juglans nigra	black walnut				◆	◆	◆	◆	◆		deciduous	rounded	medium	large
Juniperus virginiana	eastern redcedar					◆	◆	◆	◆		evergreen	columnar	medium	large
Lagerstroemia indica	crapemyrtle			◆	◆		◆	◆		◆	deciduous	vase	fast	small
Liquidambar styraciflua	American sweetgum	◆	◆	◆	◆	◆	◆				deciduous	oval	medium to fast	large
Liriodendron tulipifera	tuliptree (tulip poplar)	◆	◆		◆	◆	◆	◆	◆		deciduous	oval	fast	large
Lysiloma watsonii	feather bush			◆						◆	deciduous	vase	medium	small
Maackia amurensis	Amur maackia	◆	◆			◆		◆	◆		deciduous	rounded	medium	medium
Magnolia grandiflora	southern magnolia			◆	◆		◆	◆			evergreen	oval	slow to medium	large
Magnolia ×soulangeana	saucer magnolia	◆	◆		◆	◆	◆	◆	◆		deciduous	rounded	medium	medium
Magnolia virginiana	sweetbay magnolia	◆	◆		◆	◆	◆	◆		◆	deciduous	columnar	medium to fast	small
Malus sargentii	Sargent crabapple	◆	◆		◆	◆	◆	◆	◆		deciduous	rounded	slow	small
Malus spp.	crabapple cultivars	◆	◆		◆	◆	◆	◆	◆		deciduous	rounded	medium to fast	medium
Metasequoia glyptostroboides	dawn redwood	◆	◆			◆	◆	◆	◆		deciduous	pyramidal	fast	large

Botanical name	Common name	Growing region									Tree type	Tree shape	Growth rate	Tree size
		NW	N	SW	SP	MW	S	MA	NE	TR				
Nyssa sylvatica	black tupelo	◆	◆		◆	◆	◆	◆	◆		deciduous	oval	slow to medium	large
Olea europaea	European olive			◆	◆					◆	evergreen	vase	slow	medium
Ostrya virginiana	eastern hophornbeam	◆	◆		◆	◆	◆	◆	◆		deciduous	rounded	slow to medium	medium
Oxydendrum arboreum	sourwood	◆	◆			◆	◆	◆	◆		deciduous	oval	medium	medium
Parkinsonia × 'Desert Museum'	thornless palo verde			◆	◆					◆	deciduous	vase	fast	small
Parrotia persica	Persian ironwood	◆	◆		◆	◆	◆	◆	◆		deciduous	rounded	fast	medium
Picea abies	Norway spruce	◆	◆			◆		◆	◆		evergreen	pyramidal	medium to fast	large
Picea glauca	white spruce	◆	◆			◆		◆	◆		evergreen	columnar	medium	large
Picea pungens	Colorado blue spruce	◆	◆			◆		◆	◆		evergreen	columnar	slow to medium	large
Pinus eldarica	Mondell (Eldarica) pine			◆	◆		◆				evergreen	rounded	medium	large
Pinus nigra	Austrian pine	◆	◆					◆	◆		evergreen	oval	medium	large
Pinus pinea	stone pine			◆	◆						evergreen	vase	medium	large
Pinus ponderosa	ponderosa pine	◆	◆		◆	◆					evergreen	pyramidal	medium	large
Pinus strobus	eastern white pine	◆	◆			◆	◆	◆	◆		evergreen	oval	fast	large
Pinus taeda	loblolly pine				◆		◆				evergreen	oval	fast	large
Pistacia chinensis	Chinese pistache			◆	◆		◆				deciduous	irregular	medium	medium
Platanus mexicana	Mexican sycamore			◆	◆		◆				deciduous	rounded	fast	large

Botanical name	Common name	Growing region									Tree type	Tree shape	Growth rate	Tree size
		NW	N	SW	SP	MW	S	MA	NE	TR				
Platanus occidentalis	American sycamore	◆	◆		◆	◆	◆	◆	◆		deciduous	oval	fast	large
Populus tremuloides	quaking aspen	◆	◆			◆			◆		deciduous	oval	medium to fast	large
Prosopis chilensis	Chilean mesquite			◆	◆					◆	deciduous	rounded	fast	medium
Prunus ×cistena	purpleleaf sand cherry	◆	◆		◆	◆		◆	◆		deciduous	rounded	medium to fast	small
Prunus mexicana	Mexican plum			◆	◆		◆				deciduous	rounded	slow	medium
Prunus serrulata 'Kanzan'	Kanzan cherry	◆	◆		◆	◆	◆	◆	◆		deciduous	vase	medium	medium
Prunus ×yedoensis	Yoshino cherry	◆	◆		◆	◆	◆	◆			deciduous	rounded	medium	large
Pseudotsuga menziesii	Douglasfir	◆	◆		◆	◆					evergreen	pyramidal	medium	large
Ptelea trifoliata	hoptree			◆	◆	◆	◆	◆			deciduous	rounded	slow to medium	small
Pterocarya stenoptera	Chinese wingnut			◆	◆		◆				deciduous	rounded	fast	large
Quercus agrifolia	coast live oak			◆							deciduous	rounded	medium to fast	large
Quercus alba	white oak					◆	◆	◆	◆		evergreen	oval	slow to medium	large
Quercus bicolor	swamp white oak	◆	◆	◆	◆	◆	◆	◆	◆		deciduous	rounded	medium	large
Quercus coccinea	scarlet oak	◆	◆			◆		◆	◆		deciduous	rounded	medium	large
Quercus lobata	valley oak			◆							deciduous	rounded	fast	large
Quercus lyrata	overcup oak				◆	◆	◆	◆			deciduous	oval	medium	large
Quercus macrocarpa	bur oak	◆	◆		◆	◆	◆				deciduous	rounded	slow	large

Botanical name	Common name	Growing region									Tree type	Tree shape	Growth rate	Tree size
		NW	N	SW	SP	MW	S	MA	NE	TR				
Quercus muehlenbergii	chinkapin oak	◆	◆	◆	◆	◆	◆	◆			deciduous	rounded	slow to medium	large
Quercus palustris	pin oak	◆	◆	◆	◆	◆	◆	◆	◆		deciduous	pyramidal	fast	large
Quercus phellos	willow oak				◆		◆				deciduous	irregular	medium	large
Quercus polymorpha	Mexican white oak			◆	◆		◆			◆	semi-evergreen	rounded	fast	large
Quercus robur	English oak	◆	◆			◆		◆	◆		deciduous	oval	slow to medium	large
Quercus rubra	northern red oak	◆	◆			◆		◆	◆		deciduous	rounded	fast	large
Quercus shumardii	Shumard oak			◆	◆		◆	◆			deciduous	rounded	medium	large
Quercus suber	cork oak	◆		◆	◆						evergreen	rounded	medium to fast	large
Quercus texana	Nuttall oak				◆		◆	◆		◆	deciduous	rounded	fast	large
Quercus virginiana	live oak			◆	◆		◆	◆		◆	evergreen	rounded	medium	large
Sabal palmetto	sabal palm						◆			◆	evergreen	palm	slow	large
Salix babylonica	weeping willow	◆	◆	◆	◆	◆	◆	◆			deciduous	rounded	fast	medium
Sapindus saponaria var. *drummondii*	western soapberry			◆	◆		◆			◆	deciduous	oval	medium	medium
Schinus molle	pepper tree			◆							evergreen	vase	fast	large
Searsia lancea	African sumac			◆							evergreen	weeping	medium	medium
Simarouba glauca	paradise tree									◆	evergreen	rounded	fast	large
Sorbus americana	American mountainash	◆	◆			◆		◆	◆		deciduous	oval	slow	medium

Botanical name	Common name	Growing region									Tree type	Tree shape	Growth rate	Tree size
		NW	N	SW	SP	MW	S	MA	NE	TR				
Stewartia pseudocamellia	Japanese stewartia	◆			◆		◆	◆			deciduous	pyramidal	slow	medium
Styphnolobium affine	Eve's necklace			◆	◆		◆				deciduous	vase	medium	medium
Styrax japonicus	Japanese snowbell	◆			◆	◆	◆	◆			deciduous	rounded	medium	medium
Swietenia mahagoni	West Indian mahogany									◆	semi-evergreen	vase	medium to fast	large
Syringa reticulata	Japanese tree lilac	◆	◆			◆		◆			deciduous	oval	medium to fast	medium
Tabebuia caraiba	yellow tabebuia									◆	evergreen	oval	medium	small
Taxodium distichum	baldcypress			◆	◆	◆	◆	◆		◆	deciduous	pyramidal	medium	large
Thuja occidentalis	arborvitae	◆	◆			◆		◆	◆		evergreen	pyramidal	slow to medium	large
Thuja plicata	western redcedar	◆	◆			◆		◆	◆		evergreen	pyramidal	medium to fast	large
Tilia americana	American linden	◆	◆		◆	◆	◆	◆	◆		deciduous	oval	medium	large
Tilia tomentosa	silver linden	◆	◆			◆		◆	◆		deciduous	oval	medium	large
Tipuana tipu	tipu tree	◆		◆	◆					◆	deciduous	rounded	medium to fast	large
Ulmus americana	American elm	◆	◆		◆	◆	◆	◆	◆		deciduous	vase	fast	large
Ulmus crassifolia	cedar elm			◆	◆		◆			◆	deciduous	oval	medium	large
Ulmus parvifolia	lacebark elm	◆	◆	◆	◆	◆	◆	◆		◆	deciduous	vase	medium to fast	large
Ungnadia speciosa	Mexican buckeye			◆	◆						deciduous	rounded	medium	medium
Vachellia farnesiana	sweet acacia			◆	◆					◆	deciduous	vase	medium to fast	small

Botanical name	Common name	Growing region									Tree type	Tree shape	Growth rate	Tree size
		NW	N	SW	SP	MW	S	MA	NE	TR				
Viburnum prunifolium	blackhaw viburnum		◆		◆	◆	◆	◆	◆		deciduous	irregular	slow to medium	small
Vitex agnus-castus	chaste tree			◆	◆		◆			◆	deciduous	vase	fast	small
Zelkova serrata	Japanese zelkova	◆	◆		◆	◆	◆	◆	◆		deciduous	vase	medium	large

RESOURCES AND CONNECTIONS

ARBOR DAY FOUNDATION

arborday.org

Founded in 1972, the centennial of the first Arbor Day observance, the Arbor Day Foundation is the largest 501(c)3 nonprofit membership organization dedicated to planting trees. More than 1 million members, supporters, and valued partners have helped the Arbor Day Foundation plant nearly 500 million trees in neighborhoods, communities, cities, and forests throughout the world to ensure a greener and healthier future for everyone.

The website has a comprehensive set of guides and extensive information about tree species, selection, planting, and care, including a zip code look-up tool that makes it easy to find your hardiness zone. Explore the Future Zone Map to see how your present hardiness zone is expected to change in 20, 40, and 60 years from now, with a toggle for moderate and severe case scenarios.

The Arbor Day Foundation's impact on the world is accomplished through our conservation and education programs, including: Alliance for Community Trees®, Community Tree Recovery®, Rain Forest Rescue®, Tree Campus Healthcare®, Tree Campus K-12®, and Tree City USA®. More information about each of these programs can be found at arborday.org.

ARBOR DAY FARM

arbordayfarm.org

This National Historic Landmark in Nebraska City, Nebraska, is the birthplace of Arbor Day, with 260 acres of natural beauty and outdoor exploration for the whole family.

LIED LODGE & CONFERENCE CENTER

liedlodge.org

Designed and built by the Arbor Day Foundation, Lied Lodge is an environmentally sustainable hotel and gathering space dedicated to supporting tree planting, conservation, and stewardship around the globe.

PLANTING CHANGE

Explore more and get involved with organizations that are creating positive change by planting trees.

BOISE, CITY OF TREES

cityofboise.org (Search: City of Trees challenge)

The City of Boise, Idaho, is working to plant 100,000 trees—one tree for every household in the city— and is challenging citizens to sponsor one seedling in the state's forests for every person in the city.

CHARLOTTE TREE CANOPY ACTION PLAN

charlottenc.gov (Search: Tree Canopy Action Plan)

Relying on community input, Charlotte's Tree Canopy Action Plan is a city-wide effort to define the vision, policies, and legal framework for trees within the city.

DALLAS URBAN FOREST MASTER PLAN

texastrees.org/projects

The Texas Trees Foundation, working with the City of Dallas and Davey Resource Group, Inc., is developing the city's first Urban Forest Master Plan, which will serve as a road map and provide detailed information, recommendations, and resources needed to proactively manage and grow the city's tree canopy.

GREAT GREEN WALL

greatgreenwall.org

The Great Green Wall is an African-led movement aiming to grow a nearly 5000-mile-long swath of trees, grasslands, and other vegetation spanning the entire width of Africa. The initiative is bringing life back to the continent's degraded landscapes, while providing food security and jobs and combating climate change, drought, famine, conflict, and migration.

L.A.'S GREEN NEW DEAL

plan.lamayor.org

Part of the Los Angeles's broad-scale program to combat climate change involves cooling the streets through tree planting efforts.

#TEAMTREES

teamtrees.org

In this fundraising campaign among hundreds of YouTube content providers and the Arbor Day Foundation, one tree will be planted for each dollar pledged, already surpassing its goal of planting 20 million trees on six continents.

TRILLION TREES CHALLENGE

1t.org

Part of the World Economic Forum's work to accelerate nature-based solutions, with a goal of conserving, restoring, and growing 1 trillion trees by

2030, this organization facilitates regional partnerships between private, public, and civil actors in the United States, Amazon Basin, Sahel/Great Green Wall, and India.

U.N. DECADE ON ECOSYSTEM RESTORATION

decadeonrestoration.org

A joint venture of the U.N. Environment Programme, the Food and Agricultural Organization of the U.N., and the U.N. Convention to Combat Desertification, this group works to prevent, halt, and reverse the degradation of both terrestrial and marine ecosystems worldwide.

OTHER TREE RESOURCES

I-TREE TOOLS

itreetools.org

These online applications based on peer-reviewed, USDA Forest Service Research, quantify the benefits and values of trees around the world.

INTERNATIONAL SOCIETY OF ARBORICULTURE

isa-arbor.com

The organization promotes the professional practice of arboriculture and fosters a greater awareness of the benefits of trees.

TREES ARE GOOD

treesaregood.org

This educational website managed by the International Society of Arboriculture provides the public with information about the benefits of trees and how to properly care for trees in the urban environment.

STATE AND PROVINCIAL MASTER GARDENER PROGRAMS

mastergardener.extension.org

Enter your state or province to discover resources and fact sheets offered by your regional extension service.

CLIMATE AND WEATHER

NATIONAL OCEANIC AND ATMOSPHERIC ADMINISTRATION

ncdc.noaa.gov

NOAA's National Centers for Environmental Information provides public access to U.S. and international climate and historical weather data and information.

U.S. DEPARTMENT OF AGRICULTURE HARDINESS ZONE MAP

planthardiness.ars.usda.gov

This website allows you to enter your zip code to find your hardiness zone and provides statewide hardiness zone maps as well.

NATURAL RESOURCES CANADA PLANT HARDINESS MAP

planthardiness.gc.ca

In addition to the plant hardiness map of Canada, this site provides maps and models that summarize the climatic requirements of thousands of plants from across North America as well as summaries about plants that occur in specific areas.

BIBLIOGRAPHY

Akers, A., J. Barton, R. Cossey, et al. 2012. Visual color perception in green exercise: positive effects on mood and perceived exertion. *Environmental Science and Technology* 46(16), 8661–8666.

American Forest and Paper Association. 2017. Our industry: fun facts. Retrieved from http://www.afandpa.org/our-industry/fun-facts.

Beckett, K. P., et al. 1998. Urban woodlands: their role in reducing the effects of particulate pollution. *Environmental Pollution* 99(3), 347–360.

Bell, J. F., J. S. Wilson, G. C. Liu. 2008. Neighborhood greenness and 2-year changes in body mass index of children and youth. *American Journal of Preventive Medicine* 35(6), 547–553.

Beyer, K. M. M., A. Kaltenbach, A. Szabo, et al. 2014. Exposure to neighborhood green space and mental health: evidence from the survey of the health of Wisconsin. *International Journal of Environmental Research and Public Health* 11, 3453–3472.

Birdsey, R., K. Pregitzer, A. Lucier. 2006. Forest carbon management in the United States: 1600–2100. *Journal of Environmental Quality*, 35, 1461–1469.

Boll, T., C. von Haaren, E. von Ruschkowski. 2014. The preference and actual use of different types of rural recreation areas by urban dwellers: the Hamburg case study. *PLoS ONE* 9(10), e108638.

Bratman, G. N., G. C. Daily, B. J. Levy, et al. 2015. The benefits of nature experience: improved affect and cognition. *Landscape and Urban Planning* 138, 41–50.

Brunson, L. 1999. Resident appropriation of defensible space in public housing: implications for safety and community. Ph. D. diss., University of Illinois, Champaign-Urbana, IL.

Capaldi, C., et al. 2014. The relationship between nature connectedness and happiness: a meta-analysis. *Frontiers in Psychology* 5, 976.

Cawley, C. G. 2011. On the atmospheric residence time of anthropogenically sourced carbon dioxide. *Energy Fuels* 25(11), 5503–5513.

Cohen, D., A. Sehgal, S. Williamson, et al. 2006. *Park Use and Physical Activity in a Sample of Public Parks in the City of Los Angeles.* Tech. no. TR-357-HLTH. Rand Corporation.

Cohen-Cline, H., et al. 2015. Access to green space, physical activity and mental health: a twin study. *Journal of Epidemiology and Community Health* 69, 523–529.

Coley, R. L., F. E. Kuo, W. C. Sullivan. 1997. Where does community grow? The social context created by nature in urban public housing. *Environment and Behavior* 29(4), 468–492.

Dadvand, P., et al. 2016. Green spaces and cognitive development in primary schoolchildren. *Proceedings of the National Academy of Sciences USA* 112(26), 7937–7942.

Daniel, T. C., A. Muhar, A. Arnberger, et al. 2012. Contributions of cultural services to the ecosystem services agenda. *Proceedings of the National Academy Sciences USA* 109(23), 8812–8819.

Denman, E. C., et al. 2015. The potential role of urban forests in removing nutrients from stormwater. *Journal of Environmental Quality* 45(1), 207–214.

Donovan, G., J. Prestemon. 2012. The effect of trees on crimes in Portland, Oregon. *Environment and Behavior* 44(1), 3–30.

Dwyer, J. F., et al. 1992. Assessing the benefits and costs of the urban forest. *Journal of Arboriculture* 18(5), 227–234.

Ellaway, A., S. Macintyre, X. Bonnefoy. 2005. Graffiti, greenery, and obesity in adults: secondary analysis of European cross sectional survey. *British Medical Journal* 331, 611–612.

Evans, G. W., J. M. McCoy. 1998. When buildings don't work: the role of architecture in human health. *Journal of Environmental Psychology* 18, 85-94.

Flouri, E., E. Midouhas, H. Joshi. 2014. The role of urban neighborhood green space in children's emotional and behavioral resilience. *Journal of Environmental Psychology* 40, 179-186.

Food and Agriculture Organization of the United Nations. 2003. Press Release. Loss of forest cover threatens freshwater supplies, FAO, March 6, 2003, Rome, FAO.org.

Food and Agriculture Organization of the United Nations. 2010. Managing forests for the future. Retrieved from http://www.fao.org/docrep/014/am859e/am859e08.pdf.

Food and Agriculture Organization of the United Nations. 2017 Watershed management. Retrieved from http://www.fao.org/forestry/communication-toolkit/76377/en/.

Food and Agriculture Organization of the United Nations. 2020. Forests and Water Programme. Retrieved from http://www.fao.org/in-action/forest-and-water-programme/en.

Fukuyama, F. 1995. *Trust: The Social Virtues and the Creation of Prosperity.* London: Hamish.

Hartig, T., P. H. Kahn, Jr. 2016. Living in cities, naturally. *Science* 352(6288), 938-940.

Hartig, T., M. Mang, G. W. Evans. 1991. Restorative effects of natural environment experiences. *Environment and Behavior* 23(1), 3-26.

Health Effects Institute. 2017. *Special Report: State of Global Air 2017.* Boston, MA: Health Effects Institute.

Kaplan, R. 1993. The role of nature in the context of the workplace. *Landscape and Urban Planning* 26(1-4), 193-201.

Kintisch, E. 2015. Amazon rainforest ability to soak up carbon dioxide is falling. *Science.* Retrieved from http://www.sciencemag.org/news/2015/03/amazon-rainforest-ability-soak-carbon-dioxide-falling.

Kirkby, M. 1989. Nature as refuge in children's environments. *Children's Environments Quarterly* 6, 7-12.

Kline, J. D., R. S. Rosenberger, E. M. White. 2011. A national assessment of physical activity in U.S. national forests. *Journal of Forestry* September, 343-351.

Knowlton, K., M. Rotkin-Ellman, L. Geballe, et al. 2011. Six climate change-related events in the United States accounted for about $14 billion in lost lives and health costs. *Health Affairs* 30, 2167-2176.

Kuo, F. E., W. C. Sullivan. 2001. Aggression and violence in the inner city: effects of environment via mental fatigue. *Environment and Behavior* 33(4), 543-571.

Kuo, F. E., W. C. Sullivan. 2001. Environment and crime in the inner city: Does vegetation reduce crime? *Environment and Behavior* 33(3), 343-367.

Kuo, F. E., A. F. Taylor. 2004. A potential natural treatment for attention-deficit/hyperactivity disorder: evidence from a national study. *American Journal of Public Health* 94(9), 1580-1586.

Kuo, F. E., W. C. Sullivan, R. L. Coley, et al. 1998. Fertile ground for community: inner-city neighborhood common spaces. *American Journal of Community Psychology* 26(6), 823-851.

Laverne, L., K. Winson-Geideman. 2003. The influence of trees and landscaping on rental rates at office buildings. *Journal of Arboriculture* 29(5), 281-290.

Lederbogen, F., P. Kirsch, L. Haddad, et al. 2011. City living and urban upbringing affect neural social stress processing in humans. *Nature* 474, 498-501.

Li, Q. 2010. Effect of forest bathing trips on human immune function. *Environmental Health and Preventative Medicine* 15(1), 9-17.

Lovasi, G. S., et al. 2008. Children living in areas with more street trees have lower prevalence of asthma. *Journal of Epidemiology and Community Health* 62, 647-649.

Luber, G., et al. 2008. Climate change and extreme heat events. *American Journal of Preventive Medicine* 35(5), 429-435.

Marcus, C. C., M. Barnes. 1995. *Gardens in Healthcare Facilities*. Martinez, CA: The Center for Health Design.

McPherson, G., J. R. Simpson. 1995. Shade trees as a demand-side resource. *Home Energy Magazine* 12(2).

McPherson, G., J. Simpson, P. Peper, et al. 2006. *Coastal Plain Community Tree Guide: Benefits, Costs, and Strategic Planting.* USDA, Forest Service, Pacific Southwest Research Station.

Miura, S., et al. 2015. Protective functions and ecosystem services of global forests in the past quarter-century. *Forest Ecology and Management* 352, 35-46.

NASA. 2017. Global temperatures. Earth Observatory. Retrieved from http://earthobservatory.nasa.gov/Features/WorldOfChange/decadaltemp.php.

NASA. 2018. Climate change: How do we know? Retrieved from https://climate.nasa.gov/evidence/.

National Institute of Mental Health. 2019. *5 Things You Should Know About Stress.* Office of Science Policy, Planning, and Communications. NIH Publication No. 19-MH-8109.

Nature Conservancy. 2020. Planting healthy air: a global analysis of the role of trees in addressing particulate matter pollution and extreme heat. Retrieved from https://www.nature.org/content/dam/tnc/nature/en/documents/20160825_PHA_Report_Final.pdf

Nowak, D. J., D. E. Crane. 2002. Carbon storage and sequestration by urban trees in the USA. *Environmental Pollution* 116, 381-389.

Nowak, D., D. Crane, J. Stevens. 2006 Air pollution removal by urban trees and shrubs in the United States. *Urban Forestry and Urban Greening* 4, 115-123.

Nowak, D. J., S. Hirabayashi, A. Bondine, et al. 2013. Modeling PM2.5 removal by trees in 10 U.S. cities and associated health effects. *Environmental Pollution* 178, 395.

Nowak, D. J., S. Hirabayashi, A. Bodine, et al. 2014. Tree and forest effects on air quality and human health in the United States. *Environmental Pollution* 193, 119-129.

Ogden, C. L. et al. 2015. *Prevalence of Obesity among Adults and Youth: United States, 2011-2014.* Centers for Disease Control, NCHS data brief, No. 219.

Ogden, C. L., et al. 2015. Childhood overweight and obesity. World Health Organization. http://www.who.int/dietphysicalactivity/childhood/en/.

Park, B. J., Y. Tsunetsugu, T. Kasetani, et al. 2010. The physiological effects of Shinrin-yoku (taking in the forest atmosphere or forest bathing): evidence from field experiments in 24 forests across Japan. *Environmental Health and Preventative Medicine* 15(1), 18-26.

Rainforest Conservation Fund. 2017. Rainforest's role in climate. Retrieved from http://www.rainforestconservation.org/rainforest-primer/rainforest-primer-table-of-contents/k-rainforest-role-in-climate/.

Scott, K., J. R. Simpson, E. G. McPherson. 1999. Effects of tree cover on parking lot microclimate and vehicle emissions. *Journal of Arboriculture* 25(3), 129–142.

Taylor, A. F., F. E. Kuo. 2009. Children with attention deficits concentrate better after a walk in the park. *Journal of Attention Disorders* 12(5), 402–409.

Taylor, A. F., F. E. Kuo. 2011. Could exposure to everyday green spaces help treat ADHD? Evidence from children's play settings. *Applied Psychology Health and Well-Being* 3(3), 281–303.

Taylor, A. F., A. Wiley, F. E. Kuo, et al. 1998. Growing up in the inner city. *Environment and Behavior* 30(1), 3–27.

Thompson, C. W. 2012. More green space is linked to less stress in deprived communities: evidence from salivary cortisol patterns. *Landscape and Urban Planning* 105(3), 221–229.

Tsao, T. M., M. J. Tsai, Y. N. Wang, et al. 2014. The health effects of a forest environment on subclinical cardiovascular disease and health-related quality of life. *PLoS ONE* 9(7): e103231.

U.S. Census Bureau. 2011. *National Survey of Fishing, Hunting, and Wildlife-Associated Recreation*. Washington, D.C.: U.S. Government Printing Office. Retrieved from https://wsfrprograms.fws.gov/Subpages/NationalSurvey/2011_Survey.htm.

U.S. Environmental Protection Agency. 2020. Heathy Watershed Overview. Retrieved from https://www.epa.gov/hwp/learn-about-healthy-watersheds-their-assessment-and-protection#ecosystem.

U.S. Forest Service, Northern Research Station. 2014. Trees save lives, reduce respiratory problems. *Science Daily*. Retrieved from www.sciencedaily.com/releases/2014/07/140725163557.htm.

U.S. Geological Survey. 2016. Surface Water Runoff. Retrieved from https://water.usgs.gov/edu/runoff.html.

Ugolini, F., et al. 2013. *Quercus ilex* L. as bioaccumulator for heavy metals in urban areas: effectiveness of leaf washing with distilled water and considerations on the trees' distance from traffic. *Urban Forestry and Urban Greening* 12(4), 576-584.

Ulrich, R. S. 1984. View through a window may influence recovery from surgery. *Science* 224(4647), 420-421.

Van den Berg, M., et al. 2016. Visiting green space is associated with mental health and vitality: a cross-sectional study in four European cities. *Health Place* 38, 8-15.

Warziniack, T., et al. 2016. *Effect of Forest Cover on Drinking Water Costs*. Denver, CO: American Water Works Association and the U.S. Endowment for Forestry & Communities Inc.

Wells, N. M., G. W. Evans. 2003. Nearby nature: a buffer of life stress among rural children. *Environment and Behavior* 35(3), 311-330.

Wolch, J. R., J. Byrne, J. P. Newell. 2014. Urban green space, public health, and environmental justice: the challenge of making cities 'just green enough.' *Landscape and Urban Planning*, 125, 234-244.

Wolf, K. L. 2005. Business district streetscapes, trees and consumer response. *Journal of Forestry* 103(8), 396-400.

Wolf, K. L. 2006. Roadside urban trees, balancing safety and community values. *Arborist News* December, 56-57.

Wolf, K. L. 2007. City trees and property values. *Arborist News* 16(4), 34-36.

Wolf, K. L. 2009. Strip malls, city trees, and community values. *Arboriculture and Urban Forestry* 35(1), 33-40.

World Bank. 2016. Forests overview. Retrieved from http://www.worldbank.org/en/news/feature/2016/03/18/why-forests-are-key-to-climate-water-health-and-livelihoods.

World Health Organization. 2016. Air pollution levels rising in many of the world's poorest cities. Retrieved from http://www.who.int.mediacentre/news/releases/2016/air-pollution-rising/en/.

World Health Organization. 2016. *Ambient Air Pollution: A Global Assessment of Exposure and Burden of Disease*. Geneva, Switzerland: WHO Document Production Services.

World Health Organization. 2017. Physical activity. Retrieved from http://www.who.int/dietphysicalactivity/pa/en/.

World Health Organization. 2017. World Health Organization's drinking water fact sheet. Retrieved from http://www.who.int/mediacentre/factsheets/fs391/en.

Xiao, Q. F., E. G. McPherson, J. R. Simpson, et al. 1998. Rainfall interception by Sacramento's urban forest. *Journal of Arboriculture* 24(4), 235–244.

Zhang, J. W., P. K. Piff, R. Iyer, et al. 2014. An occasion for unselfing: beautiful nature leads to prosociality. *Journal of Environmental Psychology* 37, 61–72.

Zheng, X., et al. 2015. Association between air pollutants and asthma emergency room visits and hospital admissions in time series studies: a systematic review and meta-analysis. *PLoS ONE* 10(9), e0138146.

FURTHER READING

Arbor Day Foundation. 2009. *What Tree Is That?* Lincoln, NE: Arbor Day Foundation.

Dirr, Michael. 2009. *The Manual of Woody Landscape Plants: Their Identification, Ornamental Characteristics, Culture, Propagation, and Uses.* Champaign, IL: Stipes.

Dirr, Michael, and Keith Warren. 2019. *The Tree Book: Superior Selections for Landscapes, Streetscapes, and Gardens.* Portland, OR: Timber Press.

Dr. Seuss. 1971. *The Lorax.* New York: Random House.

Forrest, Mary. 2006. *Landscape Trees and Shrubs: Selection, Use, and Management.* Cambridge, MA: CABI.

Gilman, Edward. 2012. *An Illustrated Guide to Pruning.* 3rd ed. Clifton Park, NY: Delmar.

Gilman, Edward. 1997. *Trees for Urban and Suburban Landscapes.* Albany, NY: Delmar.

Giono, Jean. 2005. *The Man Who Planted Trees.* White River Junction, VT: Chelsea Green.

Hugo, Nancy Ross. 2011. *Seeing Trees: Discover the Extraordinary Secrets of Everyday Trees.* Portland, OR: Timber Press.

Jacobson, Arthur Lee. 1996. *North American Landscape Trees*. Berkeley, CA: Ten Speed Press.

Johnson, J. R., G. R. Johnson, M. H. McDonough, L. L. Burban, and J. K. Monear. 2008. *Tree Owner's Manual for the Northeastern and Midwestern United States*. U.S. Department of Agriculture. Available online at treeownersmanual.info

Jonnes, Jill. 2016. *Urban Forests: A Natural History of Trees in the American Cityscape*. New York: Viking.

Louv, Richard. 2008. *Last Child in the Woods: Saving Our Children from Nature-Deficit Disorder*. Chapel Hill, NC: Algonquin.

Pollan, Michael. 1991. *Second Nature: A Gardener's Education*. New York: Atlantic Monthly Press.

Powers, Richard. 2018. *The Overstory: A Novel*. New York: W. W. Norton & Company.

Preston, Richard. 2007. *The Wild Trees: A Story of Passion and Daring*. New York: Random House.

Riley, Gretchen, and Peter D. Smith. 2015. *Famous Trees of Texas*, Texas A&M Forest Service Centennial Edition. College Station, TX: Texas A&M University Press.

Silverstein, Shel. 2006. *The Giving Tree*. New York: HarperCollins.

Tallamy, Douglas. 2009. *Bringing Nature Home: How You Can Sustain Wildlife with Native Plants*. Portland, OR: Timber Press.

TreePeople, with Andy and Katie Lipkis. 1990. *The Simple Act of Planting a Tree: A Citizen Forester's Guide to Healing Your Neighborhood, Your City, and Your World*. Los Angeles: J.P. Tarcher.

Urban, James. 2008. *Up by Roots: Healthy Soils and Trees in the Built Environment*. Atlanta, GA: International Society for Arboriculture.

Watson, Gary, and E. B. Himelick. 2013. *The Practical Science of Planting Trees*. Atlanta, GA: International Society for Arboriculture.

Wohlleben, Peter. 2016. *The Hidden Life of Trees*. Berkeley, CA: Greystone Books.

Worth, Bonnie. 2006. *I Can Name 50 Trees Today*. New York: Random House.

PHOTOGRAPHY CREDITS

Sam Ambler, page 50 (bottom)
Arbor Day Foundation, pages 27 (right),
  38 (bottom), 42, 47 (top), 54 (top
  right), 61 (bottom right), 90 (left), 113
Green Forests Work, page 56
Karina Helm, pages 58, 111 (top), 63
Dana Karcher, pages 47 (bottom
  right), 54 (bottom left)
Kessler Photography (courtesy of Arbor
  Day Foundation), page 45
Lambe family photo, page 13
Land Life Company, page 61 (top)
The Morton Arboretum, page 165
Robbie Searcy, page 26
Tara Inc Photography, page 97
Mitch Wiebell Photography,
  page 54 (top left)

Alamy
inga spence, page 23

Dreamstime.com
Akvals, page 16
Alan Budman, page 100 (right)
Alex Grichenko, page 80
Alexmak72427, page 73 (right)
Alice Hawks, page 91 (bottom)
Andreistanescu, page 88 (top)
Andrii Biletskyi, page 17 (bottom left)
Animaflora, page 170
Biro Csaba, page 59
Bornholm, page 66
Charles Knowles, pages 89, 126 (top)
Cheryl Davis, page 99 (top)
Chormail, page 77 (top left)

Christinlola, page 27 (left)
Christoph Riddle, page 134
Cpenler, page 25
Daniel Thornberg, page 71 (top left)
Daveallenphoto, page 22
Davidgn, page 107
Davidhoffmanphotography, page 19
Denis Shipunov, page 78 (bottom right)
Deymos, page 99 (bottom)
Gavril Margittai, page 123
Heather Snow, page 20
Hel080808, page 126 (bottom right)
Helga11, page 110 (top)
Iva Villi, page 133
Janateneva, page 73 (left)
Jason Finn, page 17 (bottom right)
Jefferypedersen, page 103 (top)
Joe Ferrer, page 109 (top)
Katarzyna Bialasiewicz, page 77 (top right)
Kaye Barrieault, page 126 (bottom left)
Ken Woods, page 67
Komposterblint, page 88 (bottom right)
Kirshelena, page 141
Lightpoet, pages 38 (top right), 115
Littleny, page 95
Marek Uliasz, page 44
Marina Sharova, page 116
Martinmark, page 78 (bottom left)
Maxim Lupascu, page 14 (bottom left)
Melica, page 94 (right)
Meryll, page 33
Nanthicha Khamphumee, page 71 (bottom)
Natalia Golubnycha, page 163
Nikolai Kurzenko, page 130
Orangeblossom, page 54 (bottom right)
Paul Hamilton, page 129 (top)

METRIC CONVERSIONS

INCHES	CENTIMETERS
¼	0.6
½	1.3
¾	1.9
1	2.5
2	5.1
4	10
6	15
8	20
10	25
12	30
18	46

FEET	METERS
1	0.3
2	0.6
3	0.9
4	1.2
5	1.5
6	1.8
7	2.1
8	2.4
9	2.7
10	3
20	6
30	9

TEMPERATURES

$$°C = 5/9 \times (°F - 32)$$
$$°F = (9/5 \times °C) + 32$$

INDEX

ARIEL PANOWICZ

DAN LAMBE is the president and chief executive of the Arbor Day Foundation, the largest nonprofit membership organization dedicated to planting trees in the world. During his 17 years with the foundation, he has led the development of innovative programs and partnerships that expand the organization's global reach. When not working to inspire people to plant, nurture, and celebrate trees, Dan is often training for triathlons and, as a self-proclaimed "aspiring foodie," searching for his next favorite restaurant. Follow Dan's work and projects with the Arbor Day Foundation's network of collaborators on Twitter @danlambe.

MISSY PALACOL PHOTOGRAPHY

LORENE EDWARDS FORKNER is an author, editor, educator, and artist who lives and gardens in the Pacific Northwest. Lorene is the author of six previous garden books, including *The Beginner's Guide to Growing Great Vegetables* (Timber Press 2021), a garden contributor for *The Seattle Times*, and the former editor of *Pacific Horticulture* magazine. Follow her work at *ahandmadegarden.com* and on Instagram @gardenercook.